Knopp,

THE OFFICIAL MECHANICS AND PHILOSOPHIES
OF THE WASHINGTON OFFICIALS ASSOCIATION

BASKETBALL OFFICIATING

MECHANICS ILLUSTRATED

2 AND 3 PERSON HIGH SCHOOL CREWS

WASHINGTON
WOA
Officials
ASSOCIATION

PUBLISHED WITH REFEREE AND THE NATIONAL ASSOCIATION OF SPORTS OFFICIALS

WOA Basketball Officiating Mechanics Illustrated:
Two and Three Person High School Crews

Published by Referee Enterprises, Inc.,
and the National Association of Sports Officials.

Printed in the United States of America

ISBN-13: 978-1-58208-228-8

CONTENTS

INTRODUCTION

Thank you to the basketball committee members and REI staff for creating the WOA Basketball Officiating Mechanics Illustrated. Your time and effort is truly appreciated and will benefit all basketball officials throughout the state.

The mechanics and philosophies included in the Mechanics Illustrated have been approved for all levels of play by the WIAA, WOA Executive Board and the WOA Basketball Committee and are expected to be followed by all officials and local associations/boards in Washington.

The mechanics outlined by the Mechanics Illustrated are a starting point and should be adhered to in the majority of situations. The statewide observation program will be based on an official following the mechanics as outlined. With that being said, it is also understood by the WOA Basketball Committee that there may be situations not covered in the book or situations where it is necessary for an official or crew to deviate from the prescribed mechanic in order to place the crew in a favorable position to officiate. If an official/crew must deviate from the approved mechanic, they should return to the approved mechanic as soon as the game situation allows.

The WOA also acknowledges Gerry Davis Sports for their support of this endeavor. Their partnership with WOA allows us to offer a great product to our members without a financial impact to the association.

Todd Stordahl
WOA Executive Director

ACKNOWLEDGEMENTS

EDITORS
Todd Stordahl, WOA Executive Director
Steve Brown, Western Washington

EDITORIAL COMMITTEE
Steve Colby, Northwest
Kevin Erickson, Snohomish County
Mike Lloyd, Seattle
Bryan Keatley, Lower Columbia

Steve Simonson, Chelan County
Dave Van Laar, Columbia Gorge
Mike Hellman, Spokane

[2013-14]
MECHANICS CHANGES
THREE-PERSON CREWS

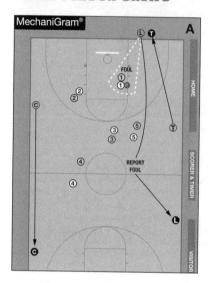

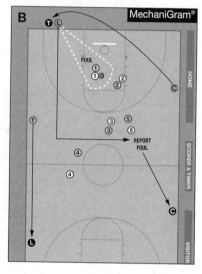

A change has been made in three-person mechanics that removes the requirement for when the lead official calls a foul and the ball is going from backcourt to frontcourt with no free throws to return to the endline and administer the throw-in.

In MechaniGram A, when a foul is called on the offense by the table-side lead and there are no free throws, there is a switch. The calling official or old lead reports the foul and becomes the new lead. The old trail moves to the endline to administer the throw-in and becomes the new trail while the center moves down court and stays the center.

In MechaniGram B, when the lead opposite the table calls a foul on the offense and there are no free throws, there is a switch. The lead reports the foul and becomes the new center. The old center moves to the endline in place of the old lead to administer the throw-in and becomes the new trail while the trail moves downcourt and becomes the new lead.

[2013-14]
MECHANICS CHANGES
TWO-PERSON AND THREE-PERSON CREWS

A tipped-ball signal has been added to the official signals to increase an official's ability to communicate with the players, coaches and fans on critical plays.

Immediately communicating whether or not the defense tipped the ball allows the offensive team to know whether or not it can recover the ball without penalty. By not giving a signal, the defense has an unfair advantage because it does not need to know which team caused the ball to enter the backcourt. It can recover the ball without penalty regardless.

MECHANICS
POINTS OF EMPHASIS
TWO-PERSON AND THREE-PERSON CREWS

Dead-Ball Officiating

See the whole play. See the actions of all players. Don't react too quickly that you do not see the second action or antics of a player that is inciting an opponent to react. Be aware of the whole situation so to penalize the correct player.

The dead-ball time after a foul, violation or timeout is critical for officials. The impact of your dead-ball officiating will affect live-ball game action. Being a good dead-ball official means a variety of things, including watching players and reporting and signaling effectively during a dead ball. After a foul or violation, it is imperative that officials perform the following duties:

• Keep all players within your field of vision. If you are the non-calling official, penetrate into the crowd slightly to let all players know you are watching. Use your voice if necessary. Don't chase the ball; going after the ball leaves players unattended.

• Communicate with your partner(s). If a timeout has been taken, indicate the spot of the ball and any other relevant information before reporting the timeout. Get together if necessary to discuss a potential problem or action and put the ball down at the spot of the inbound or free throw if you must leave that spot. Work with the table at that point to alleviate any questions or concerns before the ball becomes live.

• Free throws. Watch players on opposite lane lines as the lead and trail (or center). The officials look opposite because it is easier to see players stepping toward you and violating than it is to see them step away from you, especially when other players are blocking your view. Adjust your angles to properly cover the free-throw action. The trail is also responsible for all players outside of the three-point arc. Be especially wary of trouble players in that area as it is an ideal time for a confrontation or altercation to occur while the ball is dead. Officiate the ensuing rebounding action and make certain to penalize any illegal maneuvers. Do not allow rough play to start during free-throw rebounding action.

Proper Mechanics and Signals

The use of proper mechanics and signals are imperative to the success of the contest and the officiating team. Proper mechanics and signals will assist in communication to your partners and will aid in the effectiveness of all officials' calls.

Officials should study, emphasize and practice proper mechanics and signals with their partners and review those items in a thorough pregame conference. That will assist the crew of officials in its game preparation and will help it perform as a cohesive unit.

Commit yourself to them. Learn them from the manual; be aware of regionally approved signals and mechanics through your state association; verify them with your trainer; review them on your own; practice them in front of a mirror and at scrimmages; critique yourself on video; and attend offseason camps.

Get so comfortable with your place on the floor that rotations become second nature, necessary motions become automatic, your eyes are attentive in the right place and ideal positioning is what you do.

Work on your signals and mechanics so that where to be and how to signal comes without even thinking. Make it natural to be in the right position to see and make the right call from the right place. Begin to wonder less about whether the play is now in your primary or your partner's area. Get very good at signals and mechanics, which will allow your mind to spend more time on judgment.

What is it that will occupy your decision-making processes a majority of the time during the game? Rules and mechanics are things to work on outside your time on the court or field. Judgment then comes through experience during games and matches … with rules, mechanics and signals already an innate part of the equation.

Officials also are reminded to use non-verbal cues to communicate with your partners and assist them in their efforts. Use only approved mechanics and signals, enforce the rules of the level being played and call the game accordingly.

Non-verbal communication occurs much more often than verbal communication. For example, a block/charge foul. The calling official blows the whistle while putting a fist in the air to stop the clock and signify a foul, followed by a preliminary signal, a counting of or waving off of a basket and an indication of an upcoming free throw or where a team will be taking the ball out of bounds. Then in conjunction with verbal communication, the calling official steps to the table and demonstrates the proper signals for the foul. To that point, there has been very little verbal communication and a great deal of non-verbal "speak."

Non-verbal communication encompasses a wide variety of methodology. One such method is signaling. Signals should communicate to all entities, especially your partner(s), what has transpired as well as instructions on how the contest should proceed. Use the block/charge reference as a case in point. The sharper and more polished the signals are, the less chance

there is for confusion. If an official is lazy, too quick or not crisp enough with their signals, confusion can creep into any situation and you can all attest to the downward spiral that could follow.

Frontcourt-Backcourt
The status of the ball and players can be particularly confusing at times, but the knowledge is necessary to properly administer backcourt violations. What if the ball is in the frontcourt during a team's offensive set and is errantly thrown into the backcourt where it is first touched by that team? Easy, backcourt violation. No problem with that one. Where it can become particularly confusing is properly recognizing and understanding the exceptions that apply to the backcourt situation.

If after a jump ball or a throw-in, an airborne player, who jumped from his or her frontcourt, is the first player to secure possession of the ball and while airborne passes to a backcourt teammate, it is a backcourt violation as soon as the backcourt teammate touches the ball. It is also a backcourt violation if a team B player jumps from his or her frontcourt, while airborne gains possession of a ball (in effect, steals the ball) that had not been in team B's control and passes to a teammate in team B's backcourt. It is not a violation if the airborne player maintains possession and lands in the backcourt.

At any time (not just jump balls or throw-ins), it is not a violation if a team B player jumps from the frontcourt, while airborne gains possession of a ball (in effect, steals the ball) that had not been in team B's control and the player lands in the backcourt.

Fight Situation Protocol
In recent years there has been an alarming rate of game incident reports citing "fighting" during basketball games. This document will serve as the protocol for game officials. The scenario shall be covered in every officials' pregame meeting prior to taking the court.

Knowledge of the rules in reference to that situation is critical for three reasons: identification of individuals participating, knowledge of subsequent penalties and knowledge of how play is ultimately resumed. Beginning with the 2013-14 season, head coaches are allowed to come onto the court in an effort to break up a fight or keep a situation from escalating. Previously, the head coach could only enter the court if beckoned by an official.

Fighting can be categorized into two groups: One, the ten players legally on the court who participate in a fight situation. Two, all bench personnel, except for the head coach, leaving the team bench area during a fight or when a fight may break out.

Penalties: Direct flagrant technical fouls and disqualification to each offender, plus an indirect technical foul to the coach when bench personnel are involved in this infraction. Each foul counts toward the team-foul count, with the exception of the indirect technical foul assessed to the head coach.

1. Preventive officiating — Maintain a high degree of focus so you are not surprised when a fight may break out on the court.

2. Be a peacemaker — Step in between opposing players prior to a confrontation escalating into a fight.

3. Find a friend — Solicit the captains of each respective team to assist in addressing unacceptable behavior of teammates.

4. *Let's Get It On* — When all else fails to prevent a fight from occurring, use the following procedures:

a. The official nearest the fight should attempt to keep all other players from participating.

b. The official(s) away from the area on the court where the fight is occurring should focus their attention to the bench areas.

c. Head coaches may enter the court to assist in breaking up a fight and/or keeping his or her players from participating in the fight.

d. Officials should not attempt to physically separate the combatants. That is a liability matter. Issues with crowd control are the responsibility of game management.

e. When the fracas has ended, direct all players and coaches to their respective bench area.

f. Meet as a crew to exchange information, address penalties and discuss resuming play procedure.

g. The referee will then meet with both head coaches at the division line to explain the action to be taken.

h. The referee will then go to the scorer's table to report and ensure that all penalties are accurately documented in the official scorebook.

i. After the conclusion of the game, file a game report with your appropriate state or local jurisdiction and contact your supervisor immediately.

DEFINITION OF TERMS

The following terms are used throughout the book. Although many of the terms will seem self-explanatory, a brief review will insure complete understanding.

"A" Look — The official who has the best view of the play.

Backside — Refers to the area in the lane when a player moves away from the lead into the lane.

Balance the floor — Refers to the positions of both the lead and the trail. When the floor is balanced, the officials are near their respective sidelines. That is the normal set position in two-person mechanics. The floor becomes unbalanced when the lead moves ball side.

Ball side — Refers to the movement of the lead official when moving across the lane along the endline. The lead moves to the side of the court the ball is on in certain situations.

Center official — In a three-person crew, the wing official who is approximately in line with the free-throw line extended. The center may be table side or opposite. During transition, the center remains the center at the opposite end of the court.

Close down — Refers to the movement by the lead along the endline from the sideline toward the near lane line.

Dead-ball officiating — Activity during the time immediately after the ball becomes dead. Don't stop officiating when the ball is dead. Continue to watch the players and prevent problems.

Free-throw line extended — An imaginary line drawn from the free-throw line out to the sidelines. The area

around the free-throw line extended is a significant guideline for two-person officiating coverage and movements.

Lane line — Refers to the free-throw lane lines perpendicular to the endline which intersect the free-throw line and the endline and run parallel to the sideline. During free throws, players are lined up in lane spaces along the lane line.

Lead official — The lead official in a halfcourt setting is normally positioned outside the endline and is primarily responsible for play under the basket and in the lane area.

Lead moving to trail — Refers to the movements and changed positions of the lead during a transition play. For example, when a play moves from one end of the court to the other, the lead moves from that position to the trail position at the other end of the court.

Low block — The area along the free-throw lane line closest to the basket but not in the lane. It is usually marked on the court with a solid square or "block."

New center — Refers to the center's new position during transition. The center often remains the center when moving to the other end of the court in transition.

New lead — Refers to the official's new position during transition. The trail becomes the "new lead" when moving to the other end of the court in transition.

New trail — Refers to the official's new position during transition. The lead becomes the "new trail" when moving to the other end of the court in transition.

Open Look/Open Angle — Being in position to see between players you are officiating.

Opposite — The side of the court opposite the table side.

Perimeter area — The perimeter area is the area in a halfcourt setting away from the basket nearer the three-point arc.

Post area — The post area is around the low block and in the bottom half of the lane nearest the basket.

Post player — Post players, usually centers and forwards, position themselves in the post area. Offensive players try to "post up" defensive players in the post area to receive passes from the perimeter.

Preventive officiating — Refers to actions by officials who prevent problems from occurring by talking to players and coaches. Preventive officiating is often related to dead-ball officiating.

Referee the defense — A strategy and philosophy that has the official focusing on the defensive player's movements to correctly judge contact situations.

Screen — A legal action by a player who delays or prevents an opponent from reaching a desired position (also referred to as a "pick").

Selling the call — Placing emphasis on a call with louder voice and whistle, and slightly more demonstrative signals. Selling only occurs on close calls and should be used sparingly. It is designed to help the call gain acceptance and show the official's decisiveness.

Skip pass — A pass thrown across the perimeter from one side of the court to the other. The pass usually starts from one free-throw-line-extended area to the other free-throw-line-extended area,

"skipping" a player positioned near the top of the key.

Spacing — Distance between the official and the play. If you're too close or too far, you can't see the play clearly.

Stay deep — Refers to an official's position on the court away from the play, usually the trail in a halfcourt setting. When the trail stays deep, the trail stays out of the passing lanes and avoids interfering with the play.

Straightlining — Describes when your view of a play is obstructed by the players. You are in a straight line with the players and cannot see the play well.

Strong side — When coaches describe plays, the strong side is the side of the court where the ball is. However, in this book, the strong side refers to the side of the court that the lead is positioned on.

Switch — A dead-ball situation created when an official calls a violation or foul. After the call, there may be a change in the positions of the officials. The switch will normally involve the calling official moving to a new position on the court.

Table side — The side of the court on which the scorer's and timer's table is located.

Top of the key — The top of the key is the area near the top of the free-throw circle.

Trail official — In a halfcourt setting the trail official is positioned near the sideline opposite the lead and is responsible for perimeter play, including the outer part of the frontcourt. The trail is also primarily responsible for the backcourt.

Trail moving to lead —Refers to the movements and changed positions of the trail during a transition play. For example, when a play moves from one end of the court to the other, the trail moves from that position to the lead position at the other end of the court.

U1, U2 — Umpire 1 and Umpire 2 are the officials who do not toss the opening jump ball (the referee or referee designate does so). U1 and U2 have specific pregame responsibilities.

Weak side — When coaches describe plays, the weak side is the side of the court opposite the ball. However, in this book, the weak side refers to the side of the court opposite the lead.

Wide triangle — Refers to the three officials "staying wide" when the offense spreads out.

Wing officials — Refers to the center and trail positions, who are on the "wing."

WASHINGTON RULE EXCEPTIONS AND INTERPRETATIONS

Blood Rule
If a player is determined to have blood on their uniform (jersey, pants/skirt) the official shall stop the game and direct the head coach to:

- Replace the player within the substitution period or take a timeout if available (60-second timeout if they have one, otherwise can use a thirty-second timeout) in order to keep the player in the game.

- For a player to return to the game, the uniform item that has blood on it must be either cleaned or replaced. If cleaned and continued to be worn in the game, the coach is verifying that the uniform item was appropriately cleaned.

- Players are not allowed to remove jersey, pants/skirt in the visual confines of the playing area (10-3-6h, 10-4.1h Technical Foul). If the player(s) leaves the bench area to replace/clean the uniform, they must do so under the direct supervision of adult bench personnel.

- If the jersey is replaced the new number must be reported to the scorekeeper before the player returns to the game, the player will not be penalized.

- If the coach uses a timeout in order to keep the player in the game, the player must be ready to play at the end of the timeout period.

Closely Guarded
Boys – Only in the frontcourt: A player shall not hold the ball, dribble the ball or control the ball in an area enclosed by screening teammates for five seconds.

Girls – Anywhere on the playing court: A player shall not hold the ball or control the ball in an area enclosed by screening teammates for five seconds.

Coaching Box
The 14-foot coaching box has been adopted.

Fifth Quarter
High School
A fifth quarter may be played only by freshmen basketball squads following the regular contest. The fifth quarter is for players who were not starters and who played in three (3) quarters or less of the regular contest.

Junior High/Middle School
A fifth quarter may be played following the regular contest. The fifth quarter is for players who were not starters and played in two (2) quarters or less of the regular contest.

Guards, Casts and Braces
Guards, cast and braces do not need a letter of authorization from the WIAA provided each meets the NFHS rule specifications.

Mercy Rule/Running Clock
Beginning in the second half, if the point differential is 40 points or more, the game clock shall run continuously for the remainder of the game except for an official's timeout (5-8-2, 4), a charged timeout (5-8-3), time between quarters (5-5-1), or the administration of free throws.

The clock shall stop for free throws, once the official signals the number of free throws to the scorers' table. The clock will then restart as it would normally.

If the shot clock can run independently from the game clock, the shot clock will remain in effect. If the shot clock cannot run independently from the game clock, the shot clock should be turned off.

Once the running clock has been initiated, the clock will continue to run even if the point differential drops below 40 points.

Protests

The WIAA allows coaches to protest a misapplication of the rules. A coach may not protest a judgment call by the official. If a coach wishes to protest a misapplication of a rule, the protest must be written in the scorebook. The information should include the time, number of fouls against each player and team, number of timeouts taken and the score of the game at the time of the protest, as well as the reason for the protest. The game is then continued from the point of interruption. If there is a question as to whether it is a misapplication or judgment call, allow the protest to proceed. The school will proceed with the protest with WIAA staff on the next school day. Officials that worked the contest may be asked for more information.

Shot Clock

Art. 1 Use a 30-second shot clock for girls or a 35-second shot clock for boys.

Art. 2 Use the shot clock the entire game, including extra periods, except when 30/35 seconds or less remain in the quarter or extra period, in which case the shot clock shall be turned off. **Note:** If the shot clock cannot run independently from the game clock, the shot clock may be turned off during the implementation of the mercy rule.

Art. 3 Control a separate timing device with a horn that shall have a sound that

is distinct and different from that of the game clock horn.

Art. 4 Have an alternate timing device.

Art. 5 Start the timing device when:
  a. Ball is legally touched on a throw-in.
  b. Player gains possession following a jump ball.
  c. Player gains possession following a rebound.

Art. 6 Stop the timing device and reset it when:
  a. Team control changes from one team to the other.
  b. A foul occurs (Exception: Art. 7e).
  c. A held ball occurs (Exception: Art. 7d).
  d. A try for goal strikes the ring or flange or enters the basket.
  e. A violation by the team in control
  f. A kicked-ball violation.

Art. 7 Stop the timing device and continue time without a reset when play begins under the following circumstances:
  a. The ball is deflected out of bounds by a defensive player.
  b. A player is injured, loses a contact lens or glasses.
  c. A charged timeout has concluded.
  d. During team control as defined in NFHS 4-12, a defensive player causes a held ball and the alternating-possession arrow favors the offensive team.
  e. After a double foul, double technical foul, simultaneous foul, simultaneous technical foul or an inadvertent whistle when there is team control as defined in NFHS 4-12 and as described in NFHS 4-36.

Art. 8 Sound the shot-clock horn at the expiration of the shot-clock period. The shot-clock horn shall not stop play unless recognized by an official's whistle. When the shot clock indicates :00 but the shot-clock horn has not sounded, the shot-clock time has not expired.

Art. 9 Allow the timing device to continue during a loose-ball situation when the offense retains possession or when a field-goal try is attempted at the wrong basket.

Art. 10 Allow the game officials to make the final decision when there is doubt as to whether a score was made within the shot-clock period or whether a try for goal contacted the ring or flange. Any activity before the next live ball shall be canceled, with the exception of any flagrant, intentional or technical foul.

Art. 11 When an obvious mistake by the shot-clock operator has occurred in failing to set or reset the shot clock, the mistake may be corrected in the shot-clock period in which it occurred only when the referee has definite knowledge

relative to the mistake and time involved. Any activity after the mistake has been discovered shall be canceled, with the exception of any flagrant, intentional or technical foul.

Art. 12 It is a violation when a try for goal does not leave the shooter's hand(s) before the expiration of the shot clock or if a try for goal has been released and then the shot clock expires while the try is in the air and subsequently the try does not strike the ring or flange or enter the basket.

Ten-Second Count
High School
There is no ten-second count for girls' basketball.

Junior High/Middle School
Leagues have the option to utilize the NFHS ten-second count, rather than follow the shot-clock operations.

APPROVED UNIFORM

a. The WOA patch shall be worn centered on the left-chest pocket.

b. Standard black/white vertically striped shirt.

c. Black whistles shall be used by the entire crew (a white logo is permissible on the whistle). If a lanyard is used, it must be black.

Exception: Associations/boards may designate one week during the season to use either a pink or blue whistle in support of cancer awareness.

d. If worn, the American flag shall be on the left arm, 5" from the inseam where the shoulder and arm seams come together.

SIGNAL CHART
STARTING AND STOPPING CLOCK

Start Clock

Stop Clock

Stop Clock for Jump/Held Ball

Stop Clock for Foul

Stop Clock for Foul (Optional 'Bird Dog')

SIGNAL CHART
INFORMATION

Directional Signal

Throw-in Designation

Visible Count

Beckoning Subtitutes

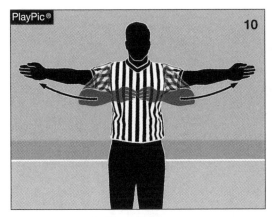

60-Second Time-out

30-Second Timeout

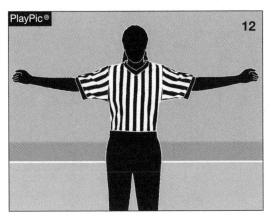

Not Closely Guarded

Tipped Ball

SIGNAL CHART
SHOOTING/SCORING

PlayPic® 14

No Score

PlayPic® 15

Goal Counts

PlayPic® 16

3-Point Attempt Score
3-Point Attempt Made

PlayPic® 17

Bonus Free Throw

PlayPic® 18

Signal Free Throw

SIGNAL CHART
VIOLATIONS

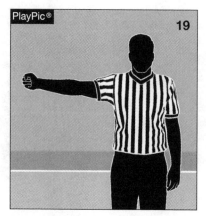

Delayed Lane Violation

Traveling Violation

Illegal Dribble

Palming/Carrying
Violation

Over and Back

PlayPic® 24

3-Second Violation

PlayPic® 25

5-Second Violation

PlayPic® 26

10-Second Violation

PlayPic® 27

Free Throw, Designated
Spot or Other Violations

PlayPic® 28

Excessively Swinging
Arm(s)/Elbow(s)

PlayPic® 29

Kicking

SIGNAL CHART
FOULS

30

Illegal Use of Hands

31

Hand Check

32

Holding

33

Blocking

34

Pushing/Charging

35

Player-Control Foul

PlayPic® 36

Team-Control Foul

PlayPic® 37

Intentional Foul

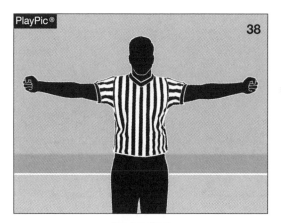

PlayPic® 38

Double Foul

PlayPic® 39

Technical Foul

3
CREW OF THREE

THREE-PERSON PHILOSOPHY

Three officials is the best way to have a game officiated. If it weren't, the NBA, WNBA, NCAA and an increasing number of high school state associations wouldn't use it. By having three officials on the court, plays that go unnoticed by a two-person officiating crew won't be. Three officials provide better court coverage than two officials because movements don't leave open gaps in coverage. Everything on the court is within the watchful eyes of the officials.

Hustle

Everyone knows hustle is needed to succeed, but what does it really mean when relating it to three-person officiating? Today's basketball games feature more speed, size and physicality than the game from 10 years ago. Three officials better control a game than two officials, but only if all three hustle.

Don't allow yourself to become lazy, thinking you won't have to hustle since there's another person on the court. That's wrong! Each official on the court has a certain set of responsibilities. If one official isn't hustling, that puts undo strain on the other two officials. When that strain happens frequently, the game suffers. Don't put your partners in difficult situations because you're not hustling.

Movements

All three officials must work hard at understanding and obtaining proper angles. Your line of sight must provide you with an opportunity to view a developing play. You must be able to see completely through the play, which means your vision must be unobstructed by the players directly involved in the play and others near the play.

Basketball is a game of nearly continual motion. An official's angle and distance adjustments are constant as play is in motion. A step or two in the right direction may open up a whole new viewing experience, free from obstruction; a step in the wrong direction will screen you from the critical game action.

Movement is needed in three-person officiating, just like in two-person crews. Unlike in two-person officiating, moving far onto the court is generally a three-person no-no. With only two officials, the trail must constantly be on the court to cover plays on the other side of the court. Not so with three officials. Almost all of the trail and center's movement will be away or toward the endlines, not toward the center of the court.

The lead also moves along the endline to improve angles. There's usually at least four and sometimes six or eight players in the lane area battling for position. Lead movement is critical to watching low-post action. It's paramount to game control.

In nearly all cases, the lead official triggers movements (rotations) by the other two officials. Well-timed, distinct movements by the lead make for smooth rotations and great court coverage.

Trust
The key to making three-person officiating successful is one simple word: trust. You must trust your partners. Only then can you concentrate on your single area of coverage and not have to worry about what's going on in someone else's area.

Understanding of court coverage
Proper coverage is enhanced by good eye contact and a "feel" for where your partners are looking. You must learn about all aspects of three-person officiating to know who is covering what. Once you've mastered that, practical on-court application develops through partner communication. You've got to know exactly what you and your partners are expected to do in specific situations — then effectively communicate with your partners — to truly master three-person officiating. When you understand why angles and distance are important and how and when to obtain them, you'll find yourself in great position throughout each game.

CREW OF THREE **CHAPTER** 2

COURT POSITIONING

PREGAME & HALFTIME

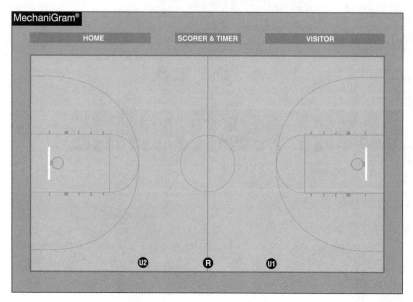

Position yourselves on the side of the court opposite the scorer's table. The referee will stand at the division line. U1 and U2 should be approximately 28 feet from the nearest endline. U2 observes the visiting team while U1 watches the home team.

BETWEEN QUARTERS

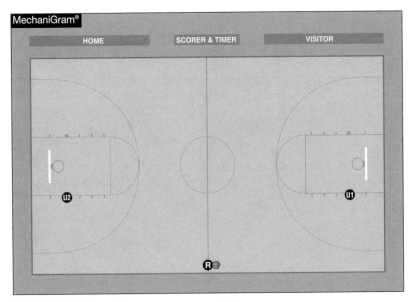

During the intermission between quarters, the officials have specific spots on the floor. While holding the ball, the referee stands at the division line on the sideline opposite the table. The umpires stand on the blocks on the lane line opposite the table facing the benches. It doesn't matter which end the U1 and U2 are on, just as long there is one official on each block.

FULL TIMEOUT

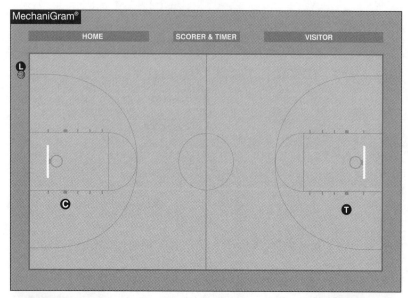

The officials assume 60-second timeout positions facing the scorer's table. The official who will be administering the ensuing throw-in will hold the ball at the location of the throw-in. The other two officials are positioned on the blocks furthest from the team benches.

At the 45-second point, you should hear the timer sound the first buzzer or horn. The officials on the blocks should take a step or two toward the team bench and give the "first horn" signal. It's a good idea to identify a person in the team bench area during pregame who is responsible for seeing that signal — assistant coach, trainer, playing captain, etc.

FULL TIMEOUT: THROW-IN NEAR BENCH

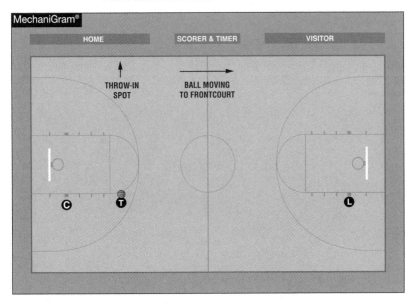

If the ensuing throw-in will be near the scorer or team benches, having the official who is to administer the throw-in standing at the spot invites problems. Instead, move straight out on the court in line with the other two officials. The other two officials are positioned on the blocks furthest from the team benches.

THIRTY-SECOND TIMEOUT

MechaniGram®

| HOME | SCORER & TIMER | VISITOR |

"Start the clock"

"First horn"

The officials assume 30-second timeout positions facing the scorer's table. The official who will be administering the ensuing throw-in will hold the ball at the location of the throw-in. The other two officials stand at the top of the near three-point arc, on both halves of the court.

At the 15-second mark, you should hear the timer sound the first buzzer or horn. The officials who are at the top of the three-point arc should take a step or two toward the team bench and give the "first horn" signal.

CREW OF THREE

THIRTY-SECOND TIMEOUT: THROW-IN NEAR BENCH

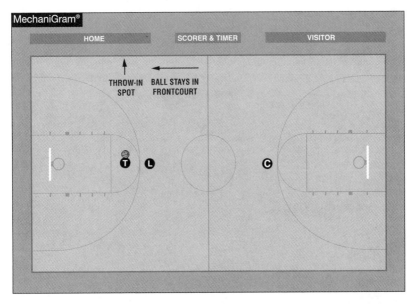

If the ensuing throw-in will be near the scorer or team benches, move straight out on the court in line with the other two officials. The other two officials stand at the top of the near three-point arc, on both halves of the court.

LEAVING AT HALFTIME

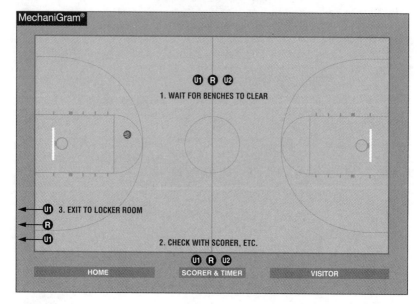

The officials are positioned halfway between the farthest point of the center circle and the sideline opposite the scorer's table (1). After both teams have left their benches and gone to their respective locker rooms, all three officials walk over to the scorer's table and the referee takes care of specified duties (2). After performing duties at the scorer's table, the officials leave together for their locker room (3).

CREW OF THREE

CREW OF THREE **CHAPTER** **3**

JUMP BALL

AFTER INTRODUCTION, BEFORE TIP-OFF

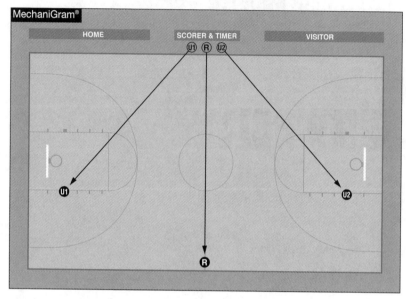

After the national anthem and the introductions of the players, the players are usually getting last words of instruction before going out onto the court. At that time, the officials should leave their positions at the scorer's table and go to specific locations on the court. The referee takes the ball and moves to a spot near the far sideline, facing the scorer's table. U1 and U2 go to the blocks opposite the team benches. Hold those positions until both teams start to come onto the court. As both teams are coming onto the court, U1 and U2 can move to the proper jump ball locations and the referee can prepare for the game's opening tip.

Note: The referee can toss the jump ball or designate one of the umpires to toss if that official throws a better jump ball. Within the book, the official tossing the ball will always be referred to as the referee. Even though the referee may designate a tosser, he or she will handle all ensuing throw-ins to start the remaining periods.

POSITIONING

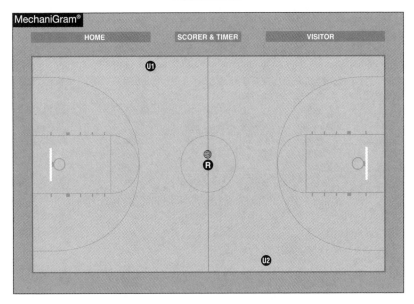

U1 takes a position on the table-side sideline, approximately 28 feet from the endline to the left of the referee. U1 is primarily responsible for calling back a poor toss, signaling the clock to start when the tossed ball is legally touched and counting the home team players. U1 also watches both jumpers.

U2 takes a position on the sideline opposite the table, approximately 28 feet from the endline and on the opposite half of the court U1 is on. U2 is responsible for the position and action of the nonjumpers and counting the visiting team players.

The referee should allow ample time for the players to get settled into their spots around the center restraining circle. While that occurs, U1 checks with the table personnel to ensure they are ready. Before entering the center-restraining circle, the referee makes eye contact with U2 first, then U1. By checking with U2 first and U1 last, if there's a problem at the table that needs immediate attention, the referee will be facing U1, making it easier for U1 to get the attention of the referee. U1 signals to the referee that table personnel and U1 are ready to go. All officials make sure the teams are facing the correct direction.

While still outside the circle, the referee notifies both team captains that play is about to begin. Tell the players to hold their spots to avoid violations. Blow the whistle with a sharp blast before entering the circle.

Before tossing the ball, you may want to use a bit of preventive officiating with the jumpers. Just before the toss, U1 uses the "do not start clock" signal (open hand raised above head). The referee tosses the ball high enough so the players tap the ball on its downward flight.

U1 and U2 must maintain a wide field of vision while the referee administers the toss.

JUMP BALL GOES LEFT

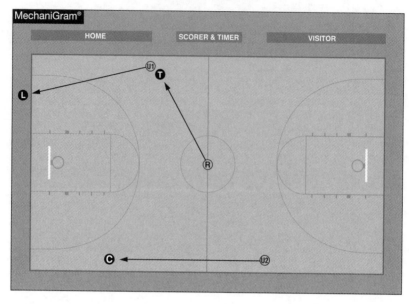

If the ball goes to the referee's left, U1 will move right and become the lead. U2 will move left and become the center. The referee will hold momentarily and then will move to the trail enabling coverage of the sideline opposite U2. U1 and U2 must be alert to move in either direction should a quick turnover occur, before the referee becomes free to move. The referee will assume sideline responsibility that U1 had during the jump ball.

After the ball is possessed, the trail should glance at the alternating-possession arrow to make sure it is pointing in the right direction. If it isn't, wait for the first dead ball and correct it.

JUMP BALL GOES RIGHT

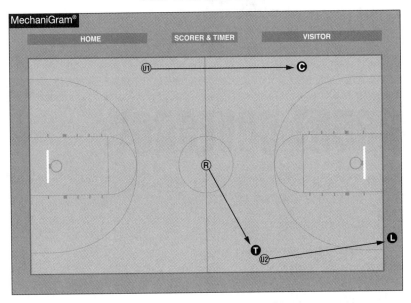

If the ball goes to the referee's right, U2 will move to the right and become the lead. U1 will move to the left and becomes the center. The referee will hold until players clear and then moves to become the trail. The referee will assume sideline responsibility that U2 had during the jump ball.

After the ball is possessed, the trail should glance at the alternating-possession arrow to make sure it is pointing in the right direction. If it isn't, wait for the first dead ball and correct it.

CREW OF THREE **CHAPTER** 4

COURT COVERAGE

HALFCOURT BOUNDARY LINE

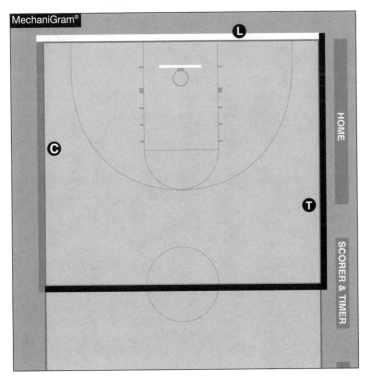

Every official on the court is responsible for particular boundary lines in a halfcourt setting. The lead and center are responsible for only one line, while the trail is responsible for two.
- The lead is responsible for the frontcourt endline.
- The center is responsible for the sideline nearest the center.
- The trail is responsible for the sideline nearest the trail and the division line.

BASIC FRONTCOURT COVERAGE

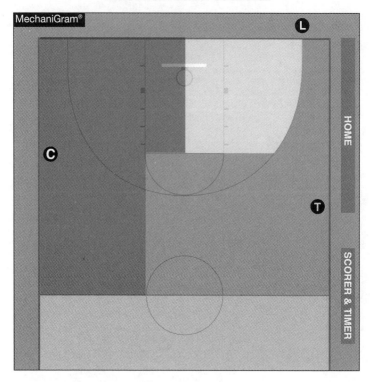

In the frontcourt, every official has a particular area of the floor he or she is responsible for. Those areas of coverage don't change regardless if you're on ball or off ball. If the ball comes into your area, you are on ball. If the ball leaves your area, then you are off ball.

Generally, in a halfcourt setting:

• The trail's responsibilities include the area to the far free-throw lane line extended, above the free-throw line, to the division line and the sideline nearest the trail. The trail also has three-point coverage on 60 percent of the court.

• The center's responsibilities include the area from the near free-throw lane line extended to the division line, the sideline nearest the center and half of the lane itself. The center also has three-point coverage on 40 percent of the court.

• The lead's responsibilities include half of the lane, free-throw line extended to the three-point arc down the to endline on the lead's side of the court.

CREW OF THREE

THREE-POINT RESPONSIBILITIES

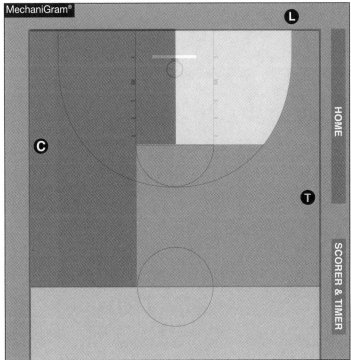

In the frontcourt, the trail is responsible for 60 percent of the three-point arc, up to the far lane line and down to the endline. The center is responsible for the three-point arc from the near lane line down to the endline. The lead does not have three-point arc responsibility except when helping in transition.

On three-point trys, only the covering official should indicate the attempt. The indication should be made with the arm closest to the center of the court so the table personnel can see it better. The covering official should also signal if the attempt is successful.

If the trail official signals a successful three-point shot, the center official mirrors the successful signal. If the center official signals a successful three-point shot, the trail official mirrors the signal. There is no need to mirror an attempt signal.

HANDLING DOUBLE WHISTLES

MechaniGram®

Double whistles are more likely to occur in areas where coverage intersects, such as in the lane, near the free-throw line and near the free-throw line extended.

There's a general rule of thumb for double whistles in the three-person system: If the play came from your primary area, you have the call.

When a double whistle occurs, first recognize that your partner(s) have blown the whistle. Give the stop the clock signal, but if all possible, do not give a preliminary signal. The outside officials (trail and center) should be patient with signals on plays to the basket as the lead tends to jump on those quickly and signal immediately.

If a drive moves into the lane area, it might even lead to a triple whistle. The reasoning: The ball originated in the trail's area so the trail stayed with the play and the center and lead picked up the penetrating player and waiting defender in the lane.

It is important to slow down, have eye contact with partners and not have a preliminary signal when more than whistle may be involved.

CREW OF THREE

PASS/CRASH IN LANE

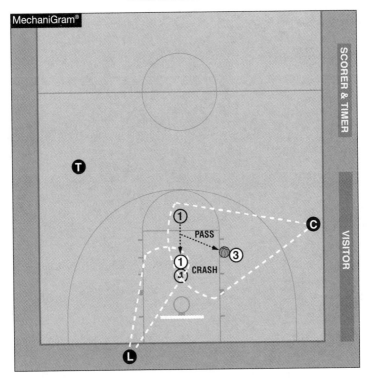

A player driving a crowded lane, passing off to a teammate, then crashing into a defender can be one of the most difficult plays to officiate. Why? There's a lot going on in a small area in a short period of time.

In a three-person crew, it becomes a bit easier because of the additional set of eyes. If the passer sends the ball out toward the trail, the trail will follow the ball and the center and lead will stay with the crash. If the ball is passed toward the center's side of the floor, the center will follow the ball while the trail and lead momentarily stay with the crash.

If you are the center or the trail official, penetrate down toward the endline to get a better view of the play, but be aware of the kickout pass and make sure you're not too close to an ensuing three-point attempt.

And as the lead official, once you determine that a drive down the lane is imminent, move toward the close-down position along the lane line (as shown in the MechaniGram) to get a better view of the activity in the lane.

REBOUNDING AREAS

MechaniGram®

Rebound coverage in a three-person crew has the same basic principles of a two-person crew. If the shot is taken from your primary area of coverage, stay with the shooter then focus on rebounding action. If the shot is taken from outside your primary area of coverage, immediately turn your attention to the rebounding action.

The third official on the court simply adds another set of eyes for rebounds. That extra set has a specific area to focus on. Those areas are very similar to basic frontcourt responsibilities, with one main difference: overlaps in coverage.

As the MechaniGram shows, there are areas on the court where two officials have the same rebounding coverage area.

While any official can call a foul during rebounding action, the trail and center officials are primary on "over-the-back," or pushing fouls when offensive players crash the boards. The lead should not call those fouls as the lead doesn't have the proper perspective the center and trail officials have. Let the wing officials make those judgments. The lead, however, can have a foul such as illegal contact or holding that is better seen from the endline.

If the shot attempts originates from the trail's coverage area, the center official becomes primary on goaltending and basket interference. Likewise, if the shot originates from the center's area of coverage, the trail then becomes primary for goaltending or basket interference.

REBOUNDING STRONG SIDE

When shots are taken from the strong side, each official has certain responsibilities.

In MechaniGram A, the shot is taken from the lead's coverage area. The lead is responsible for the shooter and strong-side rebounding. The trail should also help with strong-side rebounding. The center official is responsible for weak-side rebounding action and should work to get a proper angle.

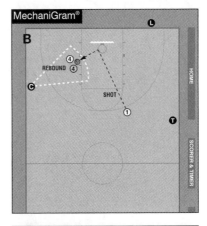

In MechaniGram B, the trail is responsible for the shooter. The center is first responsible for basket interference and goaltending, followed by observing weak-side rebounding action.

In MechaniGram C, the trail is first responsible for the shooter, followed by observing perimeter rebounding. The center is responsible for basket interference and goaltending. The center can also help with perimeter rebounding.

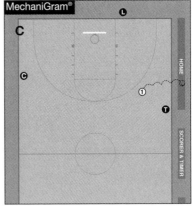

REBOUNDING WEAK SIDE

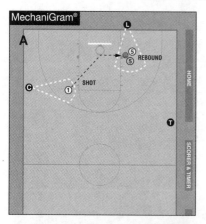

When shots are taken from the weak side, the center is responsible for staying with the shooter. The lead is responsible for strong-side rebounding, as seen in MechaniGram A.

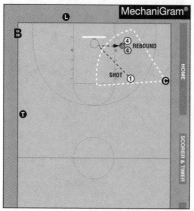

The center, after staying with the shooter, also has weak-side rebounding, as seen in MechaniGram B. The trail is primary on basket interference and goaltending and should help with perimeter and strong-side rebounding.

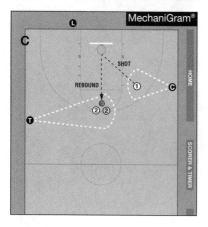

In MechaniGram C, after checking for basket interference or goaltending, the trail is then responsible for perimeter rebounding action.

CREW OF THREE

STAY NEAR SIDELINE

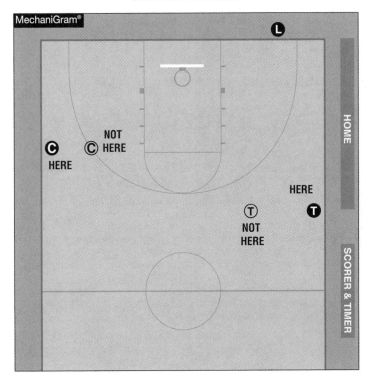

Officials learning three-person mechanics have a tendency to have a two-person mentality when on the court. One adjustment that needs to be made is where to position yourself while on the floor. In a two-person crew, the trail official must get off the sideline to properly officiate play above the free-throw line on the opposite side of the court. That is not the case in a three-person crew, as there is an official on both sidelines. Having both sidelines covered allows the trail and center officials to stay near the sideline, as seen in the MechaniGram. Staying near the sideline not only takes away the possibility of getting caught in the play, but also opens your angle of the entire court allowing for better coverage.

There may be times in which a temporary one- or two-step adjustment onto the court is necessary to avoid straightlining or feeling "pinched" along the sideline (when players are too close) or when all of the action is far away from the wing official.

DON'T BAIL OUT ON TRY

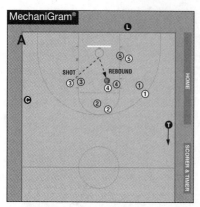

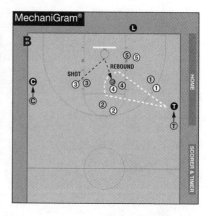

On trys, the trail and center should "stay home" and not bail out. When bailing out, as the wing official does in MechaniGram A, the wing puts pressure on the rest of the crew to officiate rebounding. Instead, the wings should step down toward the endline when trys are attempted. That helps officiate rebounding action as seen in MechaniGram B.

Force yourself to step down toward the action, particularly as the center official. While you are always searching for the perfect angle to see the action unfold, a "step down" mentality might help you to avoid bailing out.

OFFICIATING THE DELAY OFFENSE

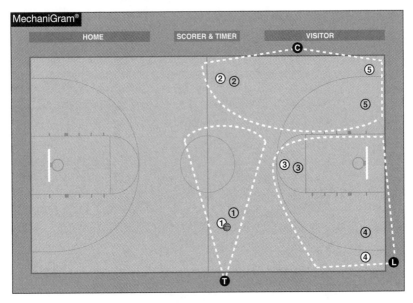

The delay offense, sometimes referred to as the "spread," presents unique challenges for officiating crews. The delay offense spreads players out to all corners of the frontcourt and is designed to run the clock down while avoiding double teams.

When a team goes into a delay offense, the wing officials may have to referee from outside the court, as seen in the MechaniGram, to keep wide triangle coverage. That way, the players have enough room to maneuver without using you as a screen. It also keeps you out of the passing lanes.

BACKCOURT BOUNDARY

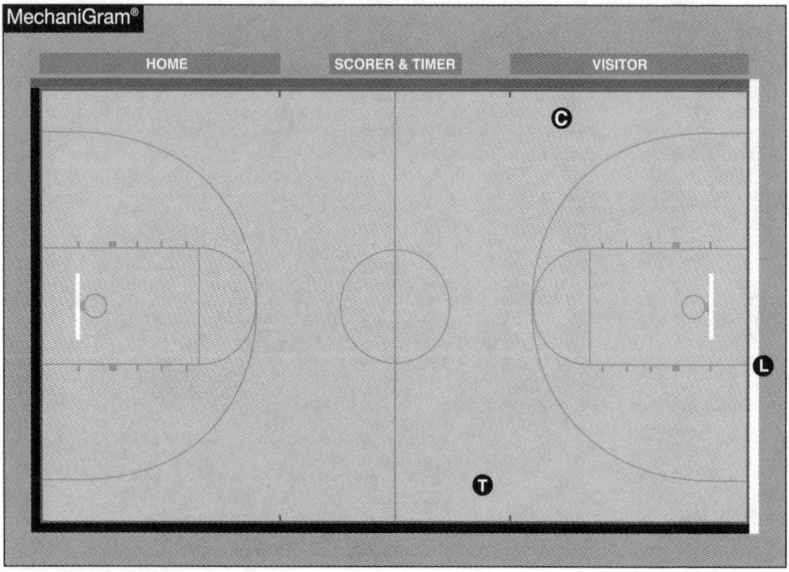

MechaniGram®

HOME — SCORER & TIMER — VISITOR

In the backcourt, the new trail is responsible for the backcourt endline and the sideline on that side of the court. The center is responsible for the sideline on the center's side of the court. The lead is responsible for the frontcourt endline.

In a pressing situation, the center official should also be prepared to help out the trail on any activity involving the division line. Many times, a quick pass to a teammate near the division line will not give the trail enough time to get up the court and get a proper angle on the play. The center is close enough to rule on any such action and penalize any backcourt violations that might occur.

CREW OF THREE

BACKCOURT NO PRESSURE

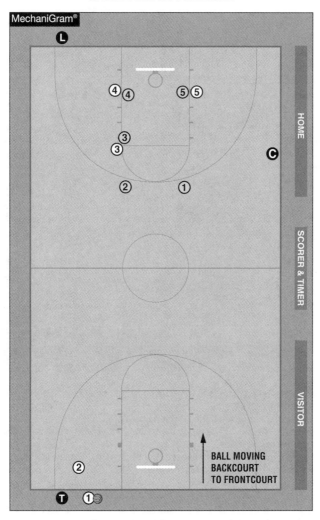

When play moves from one endline toward the other, the trail has primary responsibility in the backcourt. For example, when there is no defensive pressure, after a made basket the trail is responsible for the throw-in and watches the players move until they get to the division line. Once all players are in the frontcourt, normal frontcourt coverage areas apply.

The trail should remain behind the players at all times, even if there is no defensive pressure.

BACKCOURT WITH PRESSURE

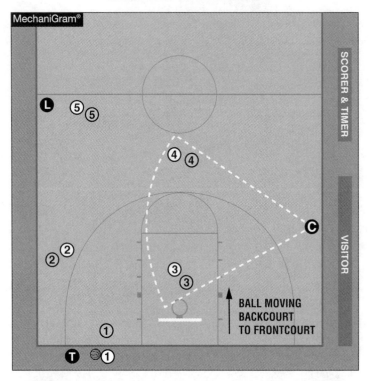

When there's defensive pressure in the backcourt, the center, and sometimes the lead, must help.

There is a general rule when the center helps the trail in the backcourt. If there are three or fewer players in the backcourt, the trail works alone there. If there are four or more players, the center helps.

When there's more than four players in the backcourt, the center's starting position is near the free-throw line extended. Basically, if you don't move after a made basket you're in perfect position. The free-throw line extended position can vary depending on the location of the players. The center must move to a spot along the sideline that gives the center the best angle to officiate. The center is responsible for the action of players in the backcourt, such as illegal screens or holding.

How long should the center "stay put" after a successful goal? Just long enough to observe there aren't going to be any problems the new trail can't handle with ease. That will probably be just a second or two. Then the center can move down the court at the same rate as the players. The lead is positioned a bit beyond the last offensive player on the court.

LAST-SECOND SHOT

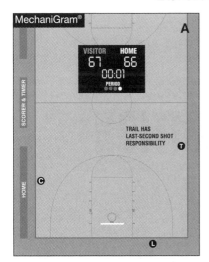

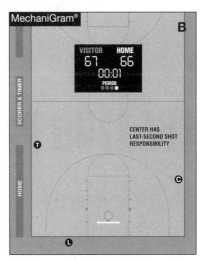

The official opposite the table, trail or center, has last-second responsibilities as seen in the MechaniGrams. That official should communicate that message and responsibility to his or her partners by signaling "I've got the shot." Such communication should be repeated on any change of possession.

If the non-responsible official has information regarding the allowing or disallowing of a basket to share with the calling official, he or she should go directly to the responsible official for a brief discussion. The referee will make the final decision in the case of disagreement or if it is necessary to consult the timer.

Last-second shot responsibilities must be discussed during your pregame so all officials know what's expected of them at that critical time.

CREW OF THREE **CHAPTER** 5

THE LEAD POSITION

- BALL-SIDE MECHANICS P. 63

- AVOID QUICKSAND P. 64

- WIDE ANGLE/CLOSE DOWN P. 65

- MOVEMENT TOWARD SIDELINE P. 66

- LEAD HELP ON THREE- POINT TRY P. 67

BALL-SIDE MECHANICS

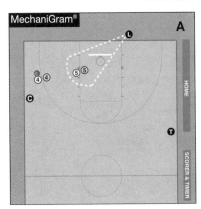

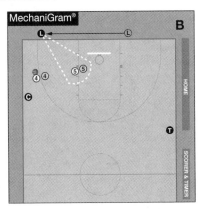

In three-person crews, the strong side would ideally be ball side at all times. While that isn't possible, the lead can move along the endline and make the strong side the ball side. The lead must anticipate a drop pass into the low post on the opposite lane line when the ball is near the free-throw line extended. In MechaniGram A, the lead is near the lane line opposite the play. It is a terrible angle to watch the post play. The lead is straightlined.

In MechaniGram B, the lead has rotated by moving across the endline to the lane line on the center's side of the court to clearly see the post play. The lead is in a much better position to see potential violations or fouls.

Keep your head and shoulders turned toward the players in the lane when moving. Remember, you still have responsibilities for watching screens and other action in your primary area. If you put your head down and sprint across the lane to the new spot you will miss off-ball contact. Move with dispatch, but move under control and with your eyes on your primary off-ball area.

The lead moves for three reasons: The lead is in a better position to see the play clearly (if the lead stayed on the off-ball side, the lead would be looking through bodies and guessing), secondly the lead is closer to the play, which helps sell the call or no-call. Perception is important and if you look like you're closer to the play and in good position, your ruling has a better chance of being accepted. Additionally, the lead will have a better view of secondary defender's on plays near the basket.

AVOID QUICKSAND

"Quicksand" is a danger area for the lead. Quicksand is the area directly underneath the basket. Never position yourself directly under the basket because you can't see much of anything from there. You're straightlined on most rebounding angles. You might as well fall into the quicksand and let your partners call the whole floor!

The lead can get caught in the quicksand when initiating a rotation and moving ball side as a player takes a shot. For example, the lead moves ball side anticipating a drop pass into the post. Instead, a shot is quickly taken while the lead is moving ball side. Now the lead must get out of the quicksand and establish good rebounding angles.

When caught in the quicksand, the lead must go back where the lead came from because the rotation wasn't completed before the shot was attempted. If you continue with the rotation during the try, your partners might not catch a rotation occurred and end up in the wrong positions.

In the MechaniGram, the lead begins the rotation and moves ball side to watch low post action. When the lead is halfway through the lane, a shot is taken. If the lead stays put, the lead is straightlined on all rebounding angles and gets caught in the quicksand. Instead, after the shot, the lead backs out where the lead is again in good position to watch rebounding action.

How does the lead know a shot is being attempted if the lead is looking off-ball? Read the off-ball players' movements. Do not watch the shooter and ignore off-ball coverage.

Off-ball players in the lane area will begin to obtain rebound positioning when a shot is airborne. Look for players watching the flight of the ball. Watch for offensive players moving to rebound spots in anticipation of a miss. Look for defensive players boxing out offensive rebounders. There are plenty of off-ball clues that let you know a shot is on the way.

WIDE ANGLE/CLOSE DOWN

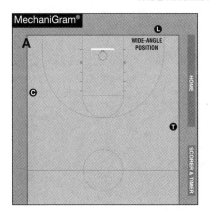

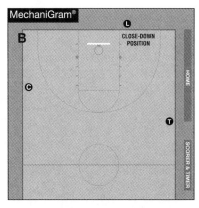

There are two basic starting positions for the lead on the endline. When the ball is on the lead's side of the court, the lead establishes a wide-angle position, which is one step inside the three-point arc line extended off the court as seen in MechaniGram A. When the ball is in the middle of the court or on the center side of the court, the lead establishes a close-down position which is three feet outside the free-throw lane line extended off the court, as seen in MechaniGram B. The close-down position makes it easier for the lead to rotate.

MOVEMENT TOWARD SIDELINE

 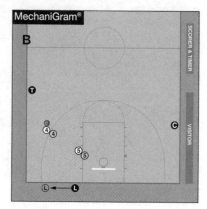

When the ball drops below the free-throw line extended on the lead side of the court, the lead's main responsibility is to watch the post players on the near low block. If you're too close to the low block, you don't have a wide angle and may not have the proper perspective.

To give yourself a wide angle and better perspective, back off the endline and move toward the sideline, work as wide as the ball. Your shoulders should not be parallel to the endline. Angle them slightly. That movement increases your field of vision and gives you a chance to see both areas.

In MechaniGram A, the lead is too close to the play and is not close enough to the sideline.

In MechaniGram B, the lead is in better position after moving off the endline, moving closer to the sideline and angling the shoulders. With that improved position, the lead has a better perspective on low block action and isn't on top of the play, which makes officiating the low-block area easier.

LEAD HELP ON THREE-POINT TRY

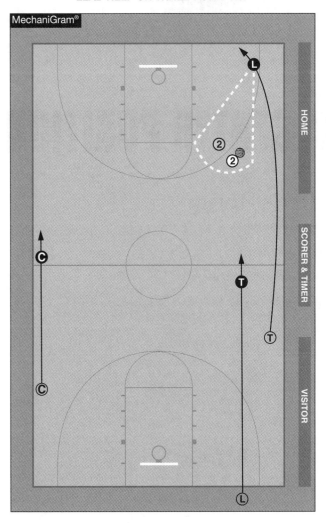

In a halfcourt setting the lead doesn't signal a three-point try or successful attempt. However, in transition that is not always the case. If a couple of passes put the ball in the frontcourt followed by a quick three-point attempt, the center and trail may not be in position to properly rule on a three-point try. In such cases, the lead can rule whether or not the try is attempted from behind the three-point arc, as seen in the MechaniGram, but should not indicate a made three-point basket.

CREW OF THREE **CHAPTER** 6

THE CENTER POSITION

RANGE OF MOVEMENT

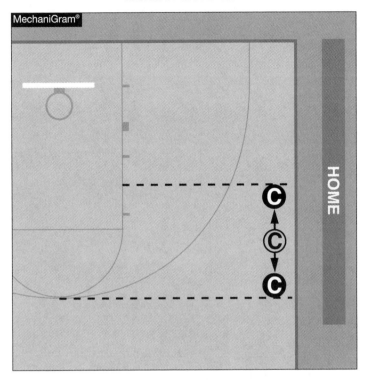

The normal starting point for the center in a halfcourt setting is free-throw line extended. That is just a starting point though and it's not the only location the center can be. The center can move comfortably up and down the sideline from the top of the key extended to the second lane space mark extended, as seen in the MechaniGram.

Movement within that range allows for the center to open angles and doesn't alter the positions or responsibilities of the lead and trail. It's the accepted range of motion for the center.

The majority of the center officials will move out toward the division line at any opportunity. It's comfortable and more like two-person. Challenge yourself to stay lower and possibly step down toward the endline instead of up toward the division line. The angles that will open up for you on off-ball coverage will be far better from that spot on the court.

MOVE ONTO COURT

When the majority of the players are on the far side of the lane, the center may need to temporarily move one or two steps onto the court, as in the MechaniGram. It doesn't do any good to have the center stay chained to sideline if there aren't any players to officiate.

By moving onto the court a couple steps, you not only bring yourself closer to the players, if you have an off-ball foul it will be easier to sell because you're that much closer to the play. While those couple of steps may not seem like a lot, the time it takes for you to cover that distance when you're trying to sell a call can be the difference between people accepting or disagreeing with the call.

When you are on the court and a play comes back toward you, simply move back to the sideline and the normal location for the center position.

OPEN ANGLES

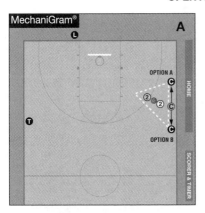

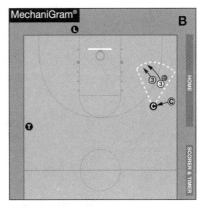

When play comes directly at the center official who is standing on the sideline, most angles and depth are lost. It is difficult to officiate any play when you have the feeling that the play is right on top of you.

The center official can and should move to maintain an open angle. Otherwise the center will become straightlined. The center can step up toward the division line or down toward the endline, as in MechaniGram A.

The same emphasis holds true when an offensive player with the ball in the center's coverage area turns the corner and drives the lane. The center must maintain the proper angle on that drive and that may mean moving onto the court a step or two to keep it, as in MechaniGram B. Officials who stay in the same place and don't move often don't see the whole play. Create the best angle.

DON'T BECOME A SECOND TRAIL

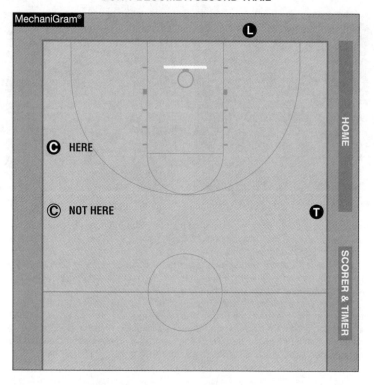

Because you're used to being above the three-point line as the trail in a two-person crew, many center officials don't move toward the endline far enough. When you're positioned too far away from the action as the center, you're defeating the whole purpose of having the third official: Better angles and better coverage.

HELP ON OUT OF BOUNDS

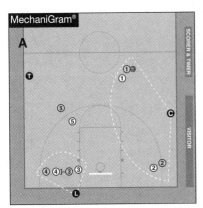 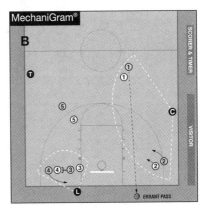

Though rare, there will be instances when action is going to occur and the calling official isn't going to know what happened. That occasionally happens on out-of-bounds calls. The center must be ready to help.

In MechaniGram A, the lead is watching a screen. The center has on-ball coverage and is responsible for the ball. In MechaniGram B, the pass is not handled cleanly and goes out of bounds on the endline.

The lead official, still watching the screen, sees the ball go out of bounds but doesn't know who touched it last. The lead should blow the whistle and immediately look to the center for help to see who caused the out-of-bounds violation. The center will know which player caused the ball to go out of bounds and should make the call.

Because the lead was watching the lead's primary area of responsibility, and with some communication by the center, the play can be called correctly, without sacrificing off-ball coverage.

SPIN MOVE

MechaniGram®

SCORER & TIMER

VISITOR

TROUBLE SPOT

A trouble spot for the lead develops when a player with the ball on the low block spins toward the middle of the lane away from the lead. The quick spin move often leaves the lead straightlined and without a good look on the play.

Many times, a defender near the free-throw line will drop down into the lane and challenge the move toward the basket. That's when you'll likely see that defender slap at the offensive player, trying to poke the ball away. That steal attempt is sometimes a foul — one that goes unseen by the now-straightlined lead.

The center must help out and watch the area in the lane when a post player spins away from the lead. Commonly referred to as the lead's "backside," the center has a much better look at the play after penetrating toward the endline for an improved angle, as seen in the MechaniGram.

CREW OF THREE **CHAPTER** 7

THE TRAIL POSITION

SPACING

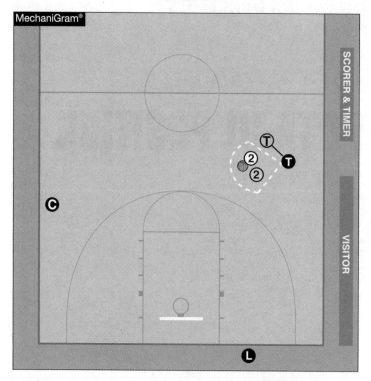

When you get too close to a play, your view of the play is distorted, as shown in the MechaniGram. Your depth perception is off and your field of vision is narrow. Also, if you're too close, you're more likely to get in the way by colliding with players or being in passing lanes. You risk impacting the play or causing injuries to the players and yourself.

When the official moves, he or she creates proper spacing and can see all of the items involved in the play (ball, defender, hands).

OUTSIDE-IN LOOK/INSIDE-OUT LOOK

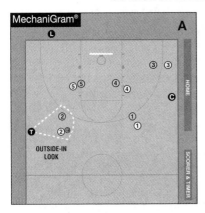

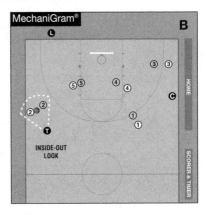

The officials in the trail and lead positions will normally referee all play in a halfcourt game on the strong side. With the ball in the frontcourt above the free-throw line extended, the trail is responsible for on-ball coverage. The trail will referee from the outside-in, assuming a position that is perpendicular to the ball whenever possible, as in MechaniGram A. Refereeing from the outside-in allows the trail to see as many of the 10 players as possible while refereeing on the ball. It allows the trail to dictate the trail's angle instead of taking the angle given by the players. When there is defensive pressure on the perimeter, before the ball clearly crosses the lane line closest to the center, the trail will step onto the court to get a better angle, or open look, on the play. Go where you need to go to see the play!

When the ball is too near the sideline, the official will move onto the court and referee from the inside-out, as seen in MechaniGram B, or up toward the division line. Once that matchup dissolves, move back toward the sideline closer to the home position. Don't stay on the court if you don't need to be.

MOVEMENT ON JUMP SHOT

MechaniGram®

SCORER & TIMER

VISITOR

SHOT

The trail has more responsibilities than simply watching the shooter. Too often a shot goes up and the trail's first thought is to start moving to the other end of the floor to avoid getting beat downcourt. When the trail leaves, the lead and center are left with offensive players crashing the boards and defensive players doing all they can to grab the rebound. That's too much to handle.

The trail must help with rebounding action. When a player takes a jump shot within the trail's coverage area, the first responsibility is to watch the airborne shooter all the way back to the floor to ensure there are no offensive or defensive fouls. While watching that action, the trail should be moving a couple of steps toward the endline, as shown in the MechaniGram.

Once everything is OK with the shooter and surrounding action, the trail steps toward the endline to allow the trail to help the lead by watching rebounding action. A step or two to improve your angle is all that's necessary to successfully watch rebounding action. Avoid going below the free-throw line extended. The trail is likely to see an offensive player pushing (or crashing into) a defensive player from behind — something that is difficult for the lead to see from the endline.

Do the game, your partner and yourself a favor and resist the urge to sprint to the other end of the floor when the shot goes up. Move toward the endline to get rebounding angles.

CREW OF THREE

CONCENTRATE ON OFF BALL

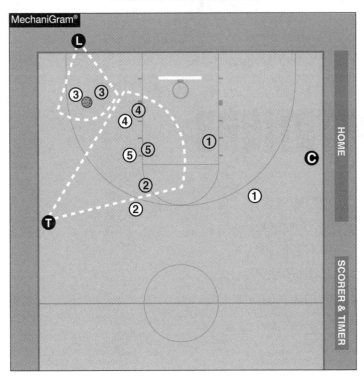

One of the many keys to successful three-person officiating is knowing when to watch off ball and when not to. When the ball is not in your primary area, you must concentrate on off-ball action.

In the MechaniGram, the lead has on-ball coverage. The trail must concentrate off ball and observe the actions of players away from the ball. If the trail were to watch the ball while it is in the lead's primary area, that leaves only the center to watch the other eight players. While that is the case in two-person mechanics, having that mindset with three officials totally defeats the purpose of the third official. Concentrate on players off the ball when the ball is out of your primary.

CREW OF THREE **CHAPTER**

8

ROTATIONS

CLOSE DOWN

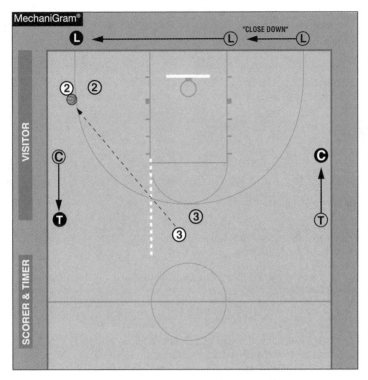

As a guideline and depending on playing action, the lead should close down and may move laterally to ball side when the ball is near the free-throw lane line extended nearest the center official. When the lead moves laterally across the endline (initiates a rotation), activity in the lane must still be observed by the lead.

"Close down" means the lead moves from an area along the endline on the lead's side of the court to the free-throw lane line nearest the lead, as seen in the MechaniGram. Often, closing down means a lateral movement by the lead of a few feet.

CREW OF THREE

WHEN TO ROTATE

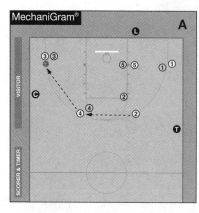

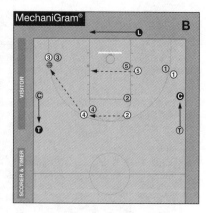

The lead should rotate when the ball is <u>near</u> the free-throw lane line extended in the center's coverage area. Remember, that is a guideline. The lead must read the playing action and anticipate ensuing plays to rotate properly, as seen in MechaniGram A.

If the ball is near the free-throw lane line extended and the lead senses ensuing post-play action (such as a post player moving ball side) as seen in MechaniGram B, the lead must initiate a rotation to get in better position to officiate the post play. By not rotating, the lead makes the center work harder by officiating a lot of action in a short amount of time.

By rotating to ball side, the lead is in a better position to officiate post action as well as secondary defender plays near the basket.

When rotating to ball side, the lead should work as wide as the ball while still maintaining focus on primary area of coverage.

CREW OF THREE

CENTER INITIATES

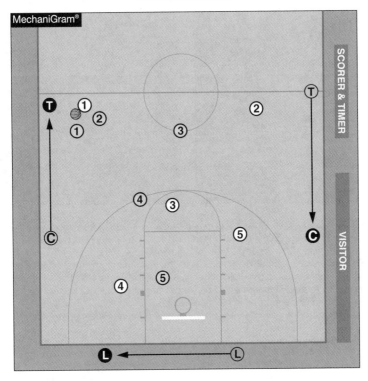

In most cases during a game, the lead dictates the rotation. However, there is a notable exception.

When a player with the ball is trapped near the division line on the center's side of the court it is a difficult area to officiate. When that happens, the center must move up toward the division line to get in better position to officiate that defensive trap, as seen in the MechaniGram. Once that happens, the other two officials must pick up on the center's movement, then rotate accordingly. With the center becoming the new trail, the trail drops down and becomes the center and the lead shifts over to ball side.

CENTER STAYS ON BALL

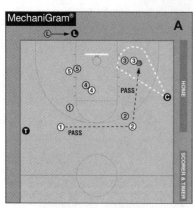 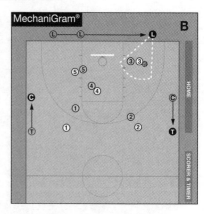

The center must referee all the action when the ball is near the free throw lane line extended nearest the center until the lead can move laterally across the floor to accept responsibility to cover the play, as seen in MechaniGram A.

The center will probably be officiating on the ball prior to any rotation for a brief period of time. In order to maintain better coverage, the center may need to pause while rotating to trail. Temporarily, there are two center officials. Complete the rotation when play permits, as in MechaniGram B.

Do not ignore the ball when it is clearly in your primary. Give it up only when you're confident your partner has picked up on-ball coverage.

CREW OF THREE

STARTED BUT NOT COMPLETED

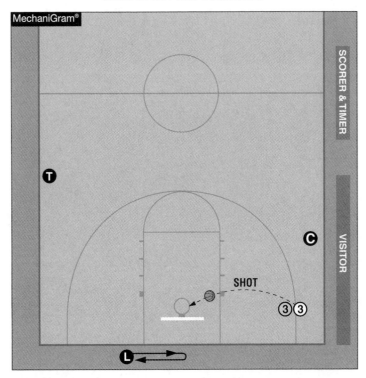

If the lead starts a rotation and then decides to stop it because of a pass or other activity, it's OK to move back to the original position because moving to the anticipated play area is most important, as seen in the MechaniGram. The wing officials (trail and center) pick up on the lead movement and swing back as well.

In either case, do not stop in the lane to officiate because of the terrible angles.

PARTNERS DON'T PICK UP

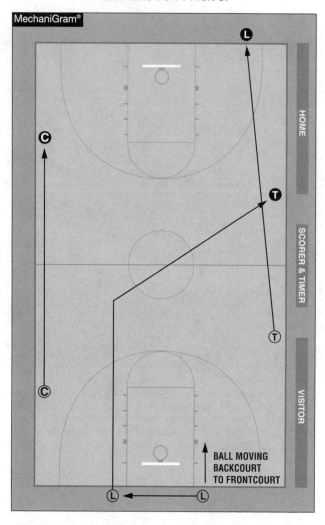

A rotation occurs, the other officials don't recognize it and, sure enough, play goes to other end of the court. Now what?

Don't panic. More times than not, the officials are the only people who know there's a mechanics mistake. The new trail must know the other officials are unaware a rotation should've happened at the other end of the court and act accordingly. The new trail must move downcourt, follow the play and simply fill in the missing gap.

In the MechaniGram, the lead rotated but the trail and center didn't see it. When play goes to the other end of the court, the old lead moves across the court and becomes the new trail.

CREW OF THREE **CHAPTER** 9

TRANSITIONS

BACKCOURT TO FRONTCOURT

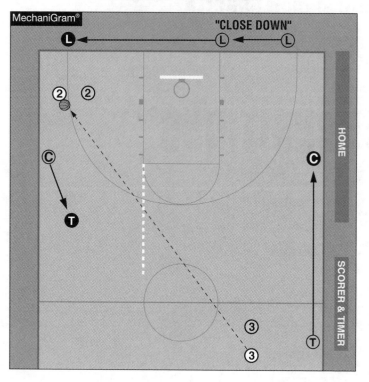

The lead may rotate ball side once all three officials or the ball and all 10 players are in the frontcourt. That makes for a smooth rotation and ensures that all three officials are aware a rotation may take place.

DON'T BAIL OUT AFTER BASKET

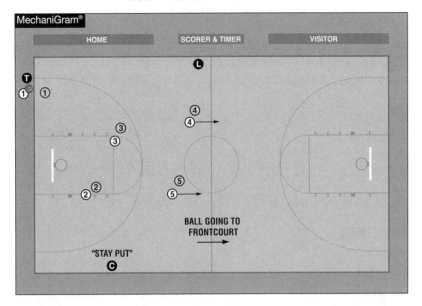

After a goal is scored, players are in a hurry to get to the other end of the court, unless the team that just scored is pressing. It is at that moment when the center can't be moving downcourt like the players.

With the center staying in the same relative location, as seen in the MechaniGram, the center helps the new trail officiate players moving to receive the ensuing throw-in pass.

If a team does press, then the center is already in perfect position to officiate the fullcourt pressure.

How long should the center "stay put" after a successful goal? Just long enough to observe there isn't going to be any problems the new trail can't handle with ease. That will probably be just a second or two. Then the center can move down the court at the same rate as the players. However, if players' actions dictate the center to stay a bit longer, do so.

TRAIL IN TRANSITION

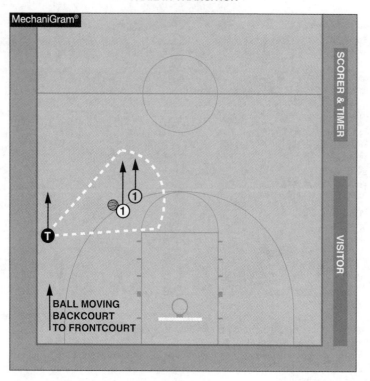

MechaniGram®

SCORER & TIMER

VISITOR

BALL MOVING
BACKCOURT
TO FRONTCOURT

Following a change in possession, the new trail should follow the players up court and be off toward the side. Don't over run the players. There's a reason the position is called the trail: You're trailing the players. The trail is responsible for all one-on-one situations until it reaches the frontcourt.

CREW OF THREE

TRAIL MOVES ONTO COURT

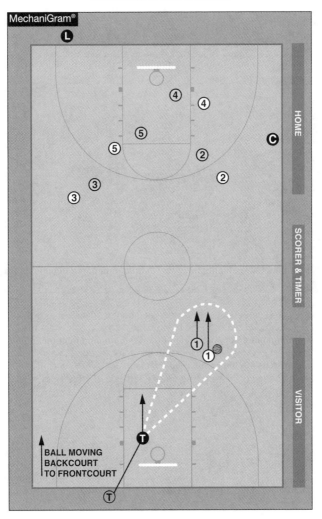

MechaniGram®

BALL MOVING BACKCOURT TO FRONTCOURT

If there is one player providing defensive pressure, the trail must move onto the court to have a clear view of the play. That may require the trail moving up the middle of the court toward the center's side to get the best angle on the play. When the ball reaches the frontcourt, normal frontcourt responsibilities apply.

AFTER A TURNOVER

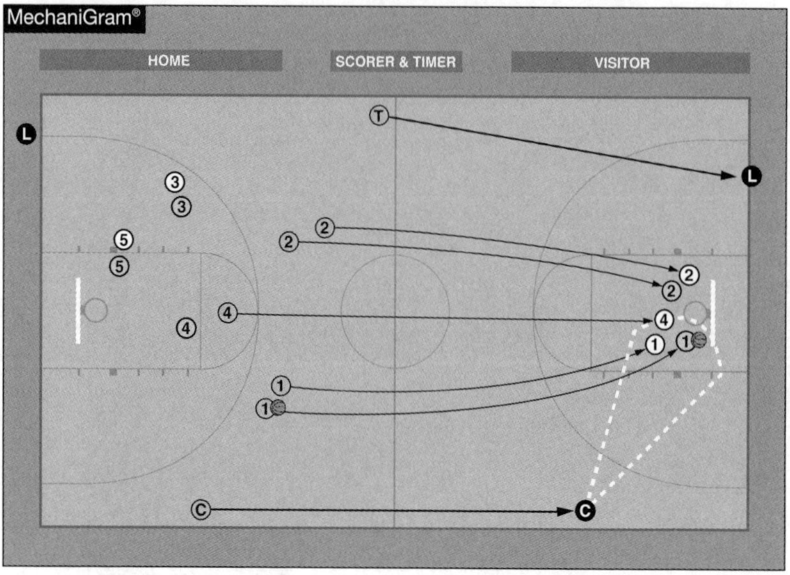

MechaniGram®

HOME | SCORER & TIMER | VISITOR

Fast break action is shared among the lead and center officials.

Much like frontcourt drives to the basket, the lead and center are responsible for action that originates from their side of the lane, even on fastbreaks. In the MechaniGram, the new lead is blocked out and can't see the drive to the basket clearly. That is the action the center must officiate.

If a play happens, move to get the proper angles and officiate as needed.

ONE-ON-ONE

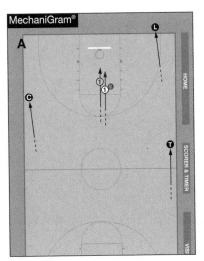
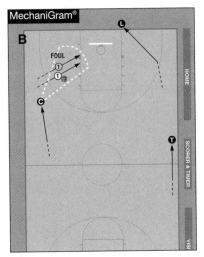

During a fastbreak one-on-one situation, the center and lead need to stay wide if the play is down the middle of the floor as in MechaniGram A. If there's a foul in the lane and a double whistle, it is the lead's call to take or give up.

In one-on-one situations, with the play originating in center's area and a foul committed on the drive to the basket, the center makes the call as in MechaniGram B. If there is a double whistle on the play, the center will take ownership of the primary area and make the call.

TROUBLE SPOT

The same pass/crash principles that apply in the lane area apply all over the court. One trouble spot for officials is the pass/crash when a team in transition starts a fastbreak up the court.

The new trail must quickly read the fastbreak and move toward the sideline. That play is the new trail's call to make.

However, if the new trail gets blocked out or can't get into a position to see the play in its entirety, the call or no-call will rest on the shoulders of the center. The center can temporarily move onto the court to help. If there's no foul or violation and play continues, the center can move back to the normal sideline position (as shown in the MechaniGram).

CENTER BUMPED

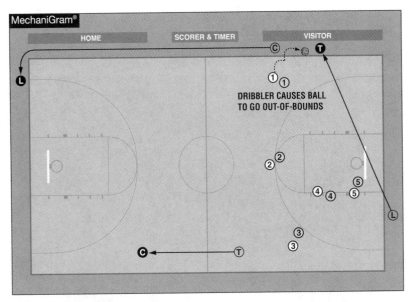

MechaniGram®

HOME | SCORER & TIMER | VISITOR

DRIBBLER CAUSES BALL
TO GO OUT-OF-BOUNDS

As the center official, when an offensive violation occurs in your coverage area, stop the clock, signal the violation and the direction, then point to the spot for the throw-in. Next — after checking that there are no problems — sprint downcourt while viewing the action behind you and become the new lead official.

If you're the lead, eye the center's signals, move toward the spot for the throw-in and administer it. The lead has now become the new trail. The lead "bumped" the center downcourt and the center moving to lead goes the length of the court. The trail will move to become the new center.

The trail becomes the new center.

CENTER RESPONSIBLE FOR BALL

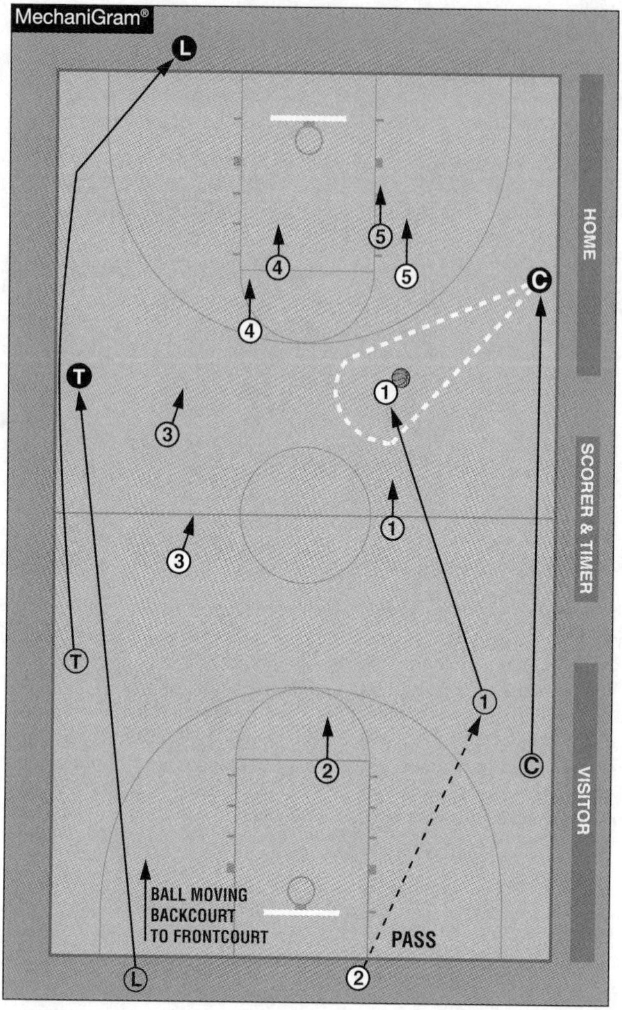

MechaniGram®

BALL MOVING
BACKCOURT
TO FRONTCOURT

PASS

HOME

SCORER & TIMER

VISITOR

If the ball is at the free-throw lane line extended nearer the center's position, the center is responsible for on-ball coverage as soon as the ball crosses the division line, as seen in the MechaniGram. Do not ignore the ball!

CREW OF THREE

LEAD CLOSES DOWN IMMEDIATELY

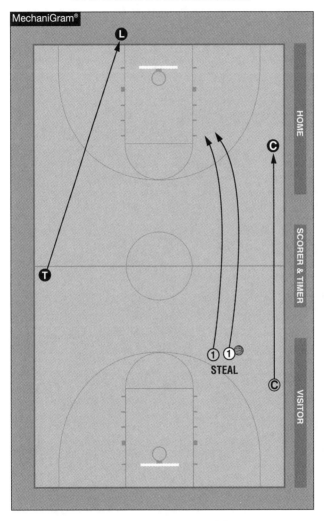

When there is a change of possession and the ball is on the center's side of the court, the new lead can go immediately to the close down position along the endline. There's no need for the lead to go to the endline, then move to the close down position. Just be sure to avoid potential passing lanes.

LEAD HELPS

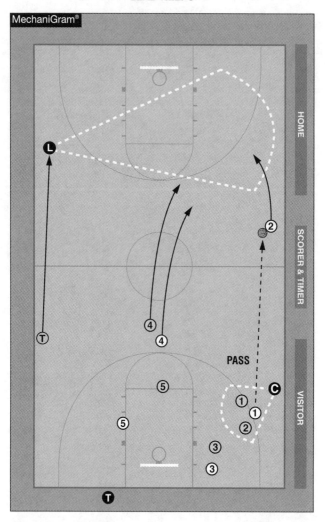

If defensive pressure is applied which causes the center to assist in the backcourt, the new lead must hesitate near the free-throw line extended or higher if necessary and assist with any action as seen in the MechaniGram. Come onto the court temporarily if necessary.

SIDELINE RESPONSIBILITY

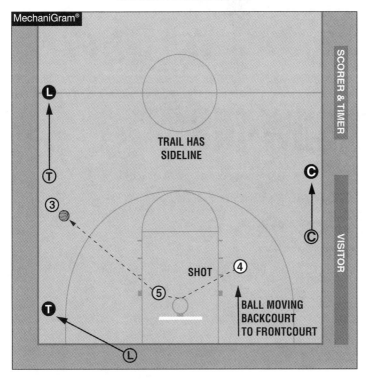

When there is a quick outlet pass after a rebound, the new trail sometimes can't cover sideline responsibilities immediately. Help is needed from the new lead. The new trail has primary sideline responsibility should the ball go out of bounds. The new lead offers secondary coverage.

If a long pass goes out of bounds downcourt ahead of the new lead, the new lead has primary coverage.

Double the sidelines in transition to help ensure your coverage will produce the correct call.

CREW OF THREE **CHAPTER** 10

THROW-INS

- ADMINISTERING OFFICIALS P. 101

- LEAD POSITION P. 102

- WHEN TO BOUNCE P. 103

- BACKCOURT THROW-IN P. 104

ADMINISTERING OFFICIALS

Which official administers a throw-in isn't any different from a two-person crew. The ensuing throw-in will be handled by the covering official. In MechaniGram A, the ball goes out of bounds on the trail's sideline. The trail is the administering official no matter how close the ball is on the sideline to the endline.

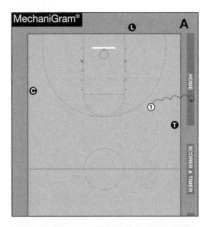

In MechaniGram B, the ball goes out of bounds on the center's sideline. The center administers the ensuing throw-in and becomes the new trail. Because two officials are needed on the same side of the court as the throw-in, the lead moves across the endline. The trail slides down to become the new center.

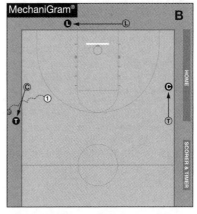

In MechaniGram C, the ball goes out of bounds on the lead's endline on the other side of the lane. The lead moves across the endline and administers the ensuing throw-in. The center slides toward the division line, becomes the new trail and mirrors the lead's chop. The trail slides down and becomes the center.

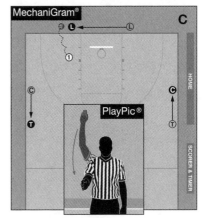

LEAD POSITION

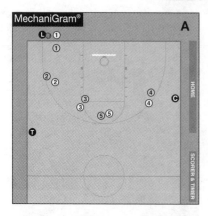
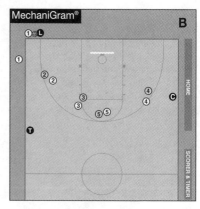

For frontcourt endline throw-ins, the lead may be on either side of the thrower, based on the best view of the play. In MechaniGram A, the lead is on the outside between the player and the sideline. In MechaniGram B, the lead is on the inside between the player and the basket. Go where you're most comfortable.

The lead should hand the ball to the thrower on all frontcourt endline throw-ins.

The trail shall mirror the lead's stop- and start-clock (chop) signals for frontcourt endline throw-ins. In many gymnasiums across the country, the timer has had a difficult time seeing the lead official chop in the clock. Having the trail official mirror the signal will give the timer additional help when the ball is in the corner and sightlines make it difficult for the timer to see the lead.

The change gives the center official increased importance. Since it's possible that two officials will now be watching the ball to initiate the chop and the starting of the game clock, the center needs to concentrate more than ever on off-ball coverage.

WHEN TO BOUNCE

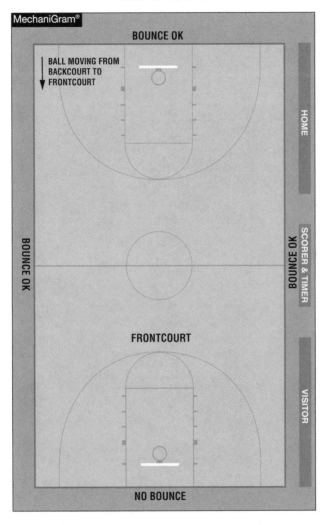

The official administering the throw-in has two ways of giving the ball to the thrower: handing or bouncing the ball. Which method depends upon where the throw-in takes place, as seen in the MechaniGram.

All throw-ins on the frontcourt endline are to be administered by handing the ball to the thrower.

Throw-ins on the sidelines or backcourt endline (with the ball moving to the frontcourt) can be done using either method.

BACKCOURT THROW-IN

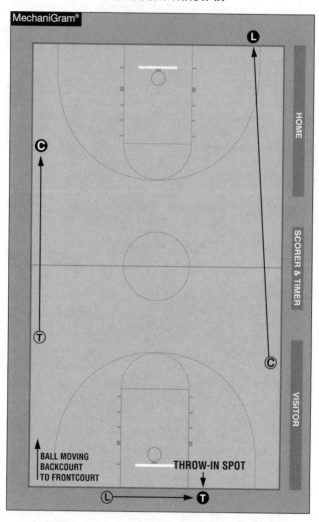

If the administering official is on the opposite side of the lane from the inbound spot, move across the lane. Do not bounce the ball across the lane. The old center moves downcourt and becomes the new lead. The old trail moves downcourt and becomes the new center. The old lead moves across the lane and becomes the new trail. Should the throw-in action cause the ball to go out of bounds on the same endline, with the same team maintaining control, the administering official may bounce the ball to the thrower-in if there is no defensive pressure in order to avoid a long switch.

CREW OF THREE **CHAPTER**

11

REPORTING FOULS & SWITCHING

FOUL REPORTING AREA

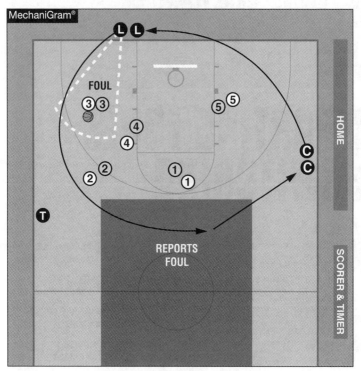

In the MechaniGram, the lead official has called a foul on the defender in the low post. At that time, the lead must do a number of things:

1. Delay momentarily after signaling the foul at the spot to ensure there is no continuing action or trash-talk among the players.

2. Once the immediate area appears calm, the lead clears all the players by running around them toward the reporting area. Do not run through a crowd because then players are behind you and you lose sight of them. That's when problems occur.

3. Stop and square up to the scorer's table in the reporting area. Make eye contact with the scorer before communicating and do not get too close to the table. If you run too close to the table, you're losing the proper perspective of possible bench conduct.

The non-calling officials also have specific duties during the dead ball:

1. Keep all players within your field of vision. Penetrate toward the crowd slightly — maybe just a step or two depending on where the players are. During that dead-ball time, you can prevent many extracurricular illegal activities from brewing into bigger problems. Use your voice to let players know you're in the area. Your mere presence may stop a problem.

2. If the players appear calm, begin moving toward the throw-in spot or begin preparing players for free throws. Move slowly and with your head up, watching the players as you move. Use your voice to tell the players what's next. By having the players ready for the next play, the ball will get back in play quickly and smoothly.

CREW OF THREE

TABLE-SIDE LEAD CALLS FOUL, NO FREE THROWS

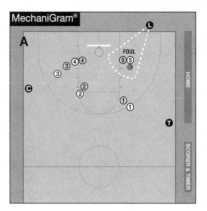
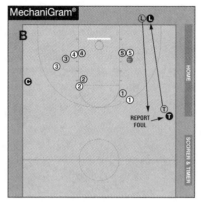

When a foul is called by the table-side lead, two officials, the lead and trail, will be involved in the switch. The lead reports the foul, stays table side and become the new trail. The old trail fills the vacated spot and becomes the new lead. The center does not switch and stays in the same position.

LEAD OPPOSITE CALLS FOUL, NO FREE THROWS

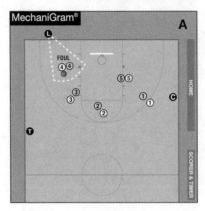
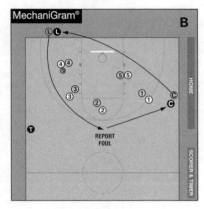

When a foul is called by the lead opposite the table, two officials, the lead and center, switch. The lead reports the foul, goes table side and becomes the new center. The old center fills the vacated spot and becomes the new lead. The trail doesn't switch and stays in the same position.

TABLE-SIDE CENTER CALLS FOUL, NO FREE THROWS

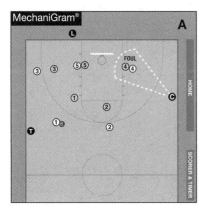

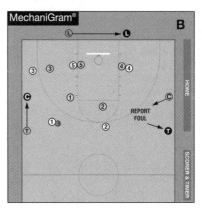

When a foul is called by the table-side center and there are no free throws, there is no switch even though all officials will be moving. The center reports the foul, stays table side, moves up and becomes the new trail. The lead stays as the lead and moves along the endline to the strong side for the throw-in. The trail slides down and becomes the new center.

CENTER OPPOSITE CALLS FOUL, NO FREE THROWS

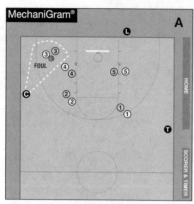
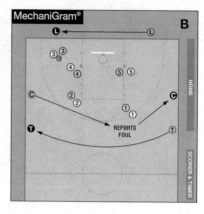

When a foul is called by the center opposite the table and there are no free throws, all three officials will be moving. The calling official, or center, reports the foul and goes table side and stays as the center even though the center is now on the other side of the court. The lead stays as the lead and moves along the endline to the strong side for the throw-in. The trail moves across the court and stays as the trail.

TABLE-SIDE TRAIL CALLS FOUL, NO FREE THROWS

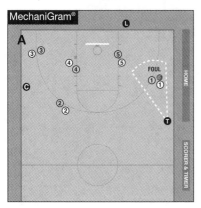
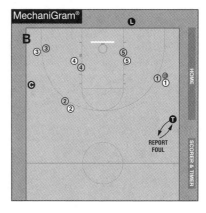

When a foul is called by the table-side trail, there is no switch. The trail simply reports the foul and stays in the same location. The center and lead officials do not move.

TRAIL OPPOSITE CALLS FOUL, NO FREE THROWS

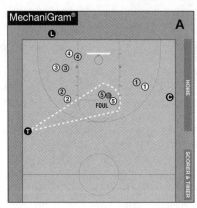

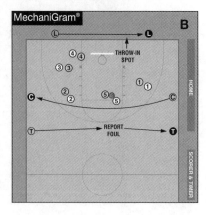

When a foul is called by the trail opposite the table and the ensuing throw-in is table side, all three officials will be moving (although only two actually switch positions). The trail reports the foul, goes table side and becomes the new trail. The old center fills the spot vacated by the old trail and becomes the new center. The lead doesn't switch. The lead simply moves along the endline to administer the throw-in but will be on a different side of the court.

TABLE-SIDE LEAD CALLS FOUL, FREE THROWS

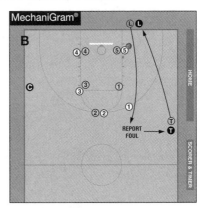

When a foul is called by the table-side lead and there are free throws, the lead and trail are involved in the switch. The lead reports the foul, stays table side and becomes the new trail. The old trail fills the vacated spot, becomes the new lead and administers the free throws. The center does not switch and stays in the same position.

LEAD OPPOSITE CALLS FOUL, FREE THROWS

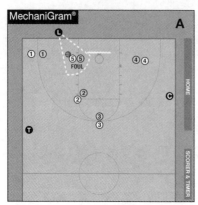 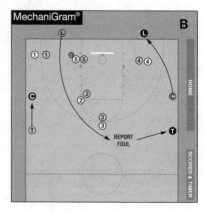

When the lead is opposite the table, calls a foul and there are free throws, the lead and center switch. The lead reports the foul, moves across the court and becomes the new trail. The center fills the spot the lead vacated and will administer free throws. The old trail stays opposite the table, slides down and becomes the new center.

TABLE-SIDE CENTER CALLS FOUL, FREE THROWS

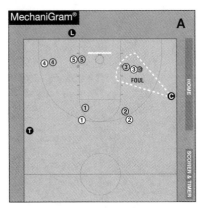

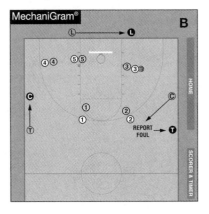

When a foul is called by the table-side center and there will be free throws, there is no switch. The center will report the foul, stay table side and become the new trail. The trail slides down to become the new center. The lead moves along the endline to the strong side, stays as the lead and administers the free throws.

CENTER OPPOSITE CALLS FOUL, FREE THROWS

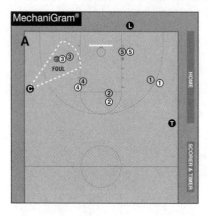
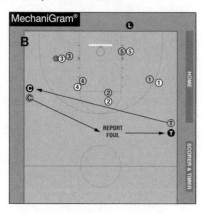

When a foul is called by the center opposite the table and there are free throws, the trail and the center switch. The center reports the foul, goes table side and becomes the new trail. The trail fills the spot vacated by the center and becomes the new center. The lead does not move.

TABLE-SIDE TRAIL CALLS FOUL, FREE THROWS

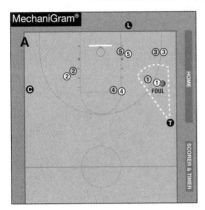

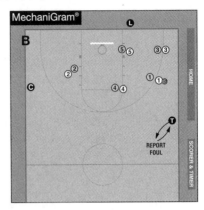

When a foul is called by the table-side trail and there are free throws, there is no switch. The trail reports the foul, stays table side and stays as the trail. The center and the lead do not move.

TRAIL OPPOSITE CALLS FOUL, FREE THROWS

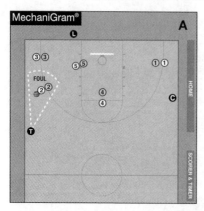

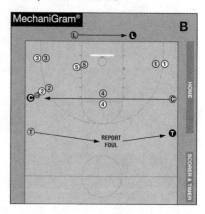

When a foul is called by the trail opposite the table and there are free throws, the trail and the center switch. The trail reports the foul, goes table side and becomes the new trail. The center fills the spot vacated by the trail and becomes the new center. The lead moves along the endline, stays the lead and administers the free throws.

TABLE-SIDE LEAD CALLS FOUL ON OFFENSE, NO FREE THROWS

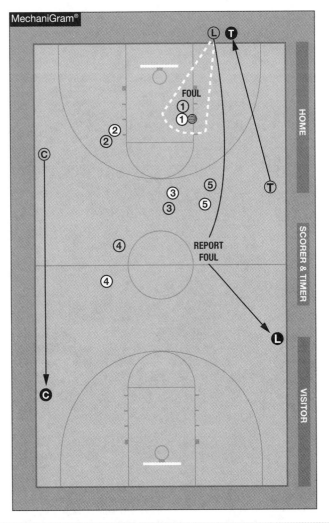

When a foul is called on the offense by the table-side lead and there are no free throws, there is a switch. The calling official or old lead reports the foul and becomes the new lead. The old trail moves to the endline to administer the throw-in and becomes the new trail while the center moves downcourt and stays the center.

LEAD OPPOSITE CALLS FOUL ON OFFENSE, NO FREE THROWS

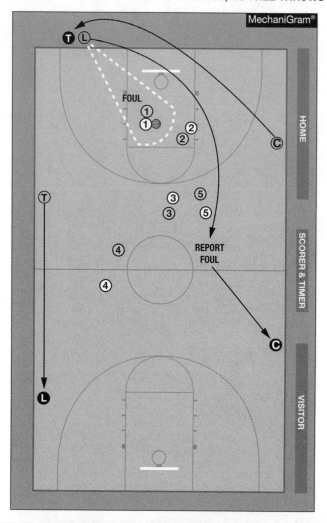

When the lead opposite the table calls a foul on the offense and there are no free throws, there is a switch. The lead reports the foul and becomes the new center. The old center moves to the endline in place of the old lead to administer the throw-in and becomes the new trail while the trail moves downcourt and becomes the new lead.

TABLE-SIDE CENTER CALLS FOUL ON OFFENSE, NO FREE THROWS

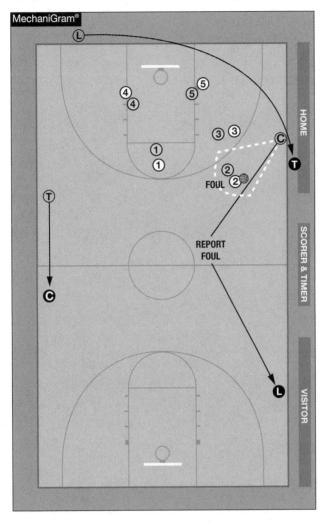

When the table-side center calls a foul on the offense and there are no free throws, the center reports the foul, stays table side and becomes the new lead. The old trail moves down the court and becomes the new center. The old lead moves across the court and becomes the new trail. The officials slide the same as they would as if a violation were called.

CENTER OPPOSITE CALLS FOUL ON OFFENSE, NO FREE THROWS

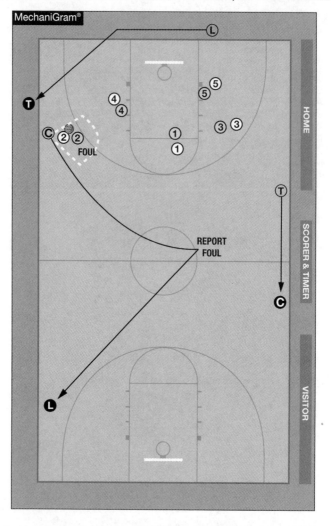

When a foul is called on the offense by the center opposite the table and there are no free throws, there is no switch. The center reports the foul but doesn't go table side. Instead, the center stays opposite the table and becomes the new lead. The old lead moves across the court to administer the ensuing throw-in and becomes the new trail. The old trail slides downcourt and becomes the new center. The officials slide as if there were a violation called.

CREW OF THREE

TABLE-SIDE TRAIL CALLS FOUL ON OFFENSE, NO FREE THROWS

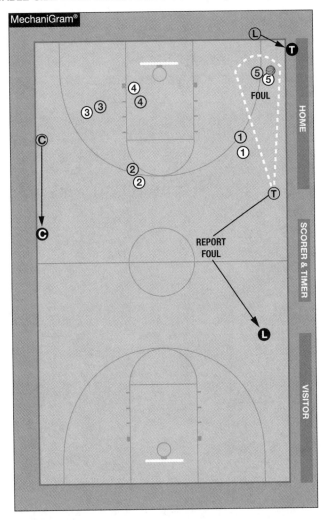

When a foul is called on the offense by the table-side trail and there are no free throws, there is no switch. The trail reports the foul, moves downcourt, stays table side and becomes the new lead. The old lead administers the throw-in and becomes the new trail. The center stays the center and moves downcourt. The officials slide as if there was a violation called.

TRAIL OPPOSITE CALLS FOUL ON OFFENSE, NO FREE THROWS

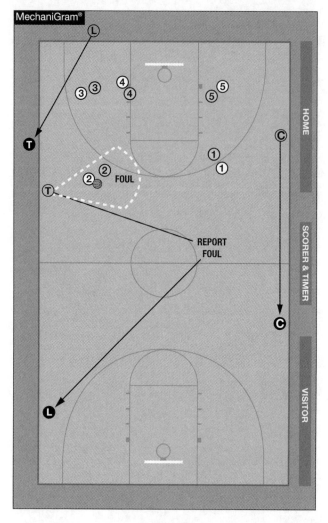

When a foul is called on the offense by the trail opposite the table and there are no free throws, there is no switch. The foul is treated like a violation. The trail reports the foul but doesn't go table side. Instead, the old trail stays opposite the table and becomes the new lead. The old lead moves to administer the ensuing throw-in and becomes the new trail. The old center slides downcourt and stays the center.

CREW OF THREE

TABLE-SIDE LEAD CALLS FOUL ON OFFENSE, FREE THROWS

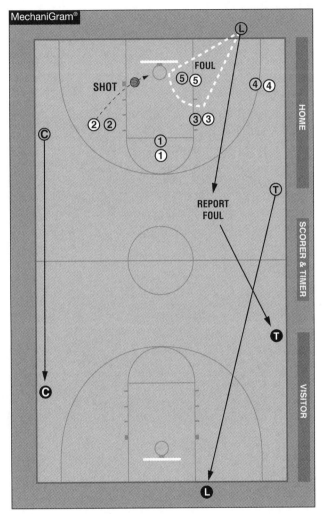

When the table-side lead calls a foul on the offense and there are free throws, there is no switch. The officials slide down the court. The lead reports the foul, stays table side and becomes the new trail. The old trail slides down and becomes the new lead. The center slides down and stays the center.

LEAD OPPOSITE CALLS FOUL ON OFFENSE, FREE THROWS

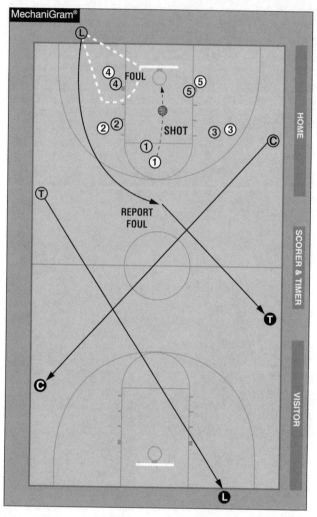

When the lead is opposite the table, calls a foul on the offensive team and there are free throws, all three officials will be moving. The lead reports the foul, moves across the court and becomes the new trail. The old trail moves across the court and becomes the new lead. The center moves across the court and stays the center.

TABLE-SIDE CENTER CALLS FOUL ON OFFENSE, FREE THROWS

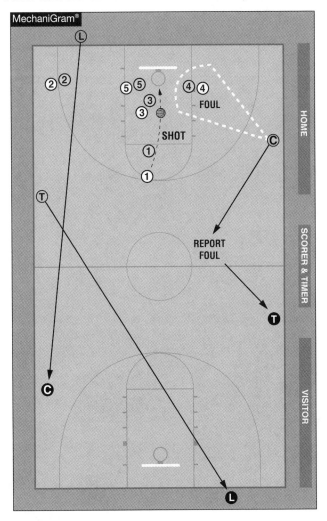

When the table-side center calls a foul on the offense and there are free throws, all three officials will be moving. The center reports the foul, stays table side and becomes the new trail. The old trail moves across the court and becomes the new lead. The old lead slides down and becomes the new center.

CENTER OPPOSITE CALLS FOUL ON OFFENSE, FREE THROWS

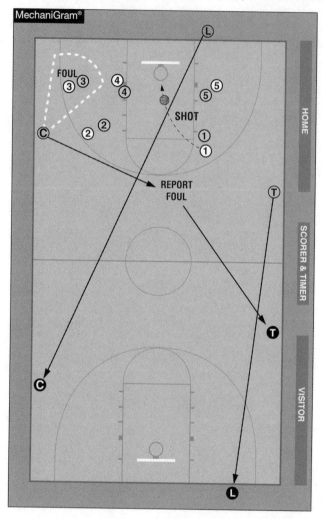

When a foul is called on the offense by the center opposite the table and there are free throws, all three officials will be moving. The center reports the foul and goes table side to become the new trail. The old trail moves downcourt and becomes the new lead. The old lead moves down and across the court to become the new center.

CREW OF THREE

TABLE-SIDE TRAIL CALLS FOUL ON OFFENSE, FREE THROWS

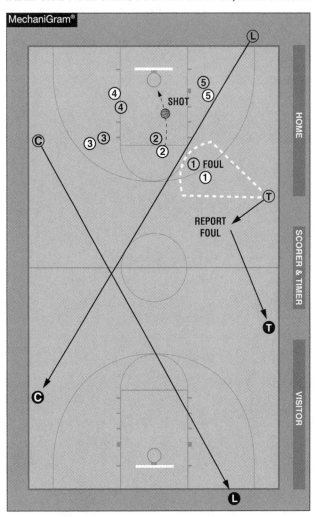

When a foul is called on the offense by the table-side trail and there are free throws, all officials will be moving. The trail reports the foul, stays table side and continues to be the trail. The old center moves down and across the court to become the new lead. The old lead moves down and across the court to become the new center.

TRAIL OPPOSITE CALLS FOUL ON OFFENSE, FREE THROWS

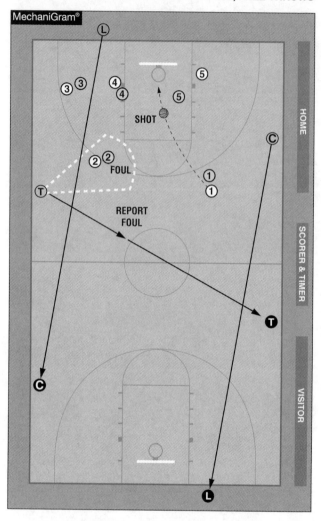

When a foul is called on the offense by the trail opposite the table and there are free throws, all officials will be moving. The trail reports the foul, goes table side and stays the trail. The old center moves downcourt and becomes the new lead. The old lead moves downcourt and becomes the new center.

NOTIFY COACH OF DISQUALIFIED PLAYER

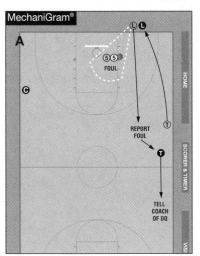
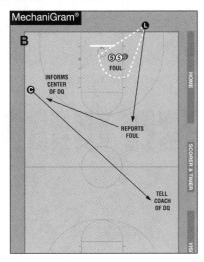

When a player fouls out, the calling official is responsible for notifying the coach, having table personnel start the 20-second substitution clock and informing the player, as in MechaniGram A.

If informing the coach of the disqualified player could be heated, the calling official doesn't have to stay table side. When informed by the table of the player's disqualification, the calling official can go opposite the table. The official who is opposite, either the trail or center, should notify the coach, as in MechaniGram B.

Any official has the same option of going opposite to avoid a confrontation, such as after a technical foul or ejection.

CREW OF THREE **CHAPTER**

12

FREE THROWS

- **COVERAGE** P. 133

- **TRAIL POSITIONING** P. 134

- **CENTER/TRAIL MOVEMENT** P. 135

- **TECHNICAL FOUL** P. 136

COVERAGE

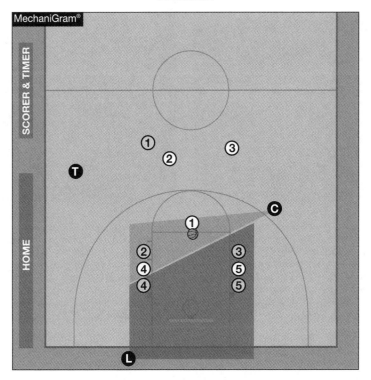

The lead official watches players on the opposite lane line (closer to the center) for potential violations, etc. The lead also watches the lane space nearest the endline on the lane line nearest the lead.

The center official observes players on the opposite lane line (closer to the lead) except the opposite low block area. The center also watches the free-throw shooter.

The trail official watches all lane activity to assist the lead and center, but also watches any action above the three-point arc.

TRAIL POSITIONING

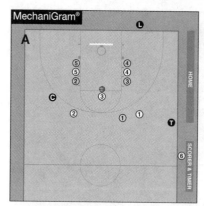 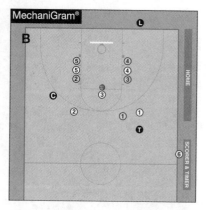

On multiple free throws, the trail shall be positioned near the 28-foot mark for the first of two (or first two of three) free throws, as shown in MechaniGram A. Take a position approximately 28 feet from the endline just inside the table-side boundary. If possible, do not obstruct the view of the scorer, timer and team benches. Be primarily responsible for holding and beckoning substitutes and any other table activity. Keep a perspective on all players in the backcourt.

If necessary to get away from a boisterous coach or volatile situation, the trail official may move onto the court, as shown in MechaniGram B.

CENTER/TRAIL MOVEMENT

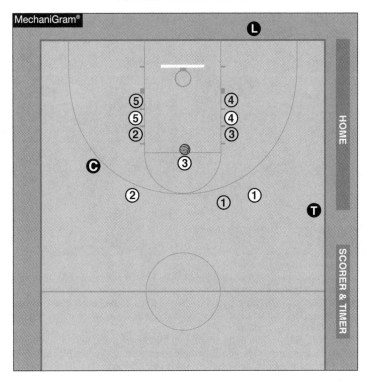

During the flight of the last free throw, the center and trail penetrate slightly toward the endline. That movement ensures good angles on rebounding action. The center is responsible for weak-side rebounding and the trail is responsible for strong-side rebounding.

TECHNICAL FOUL

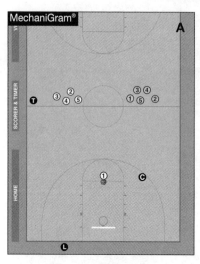

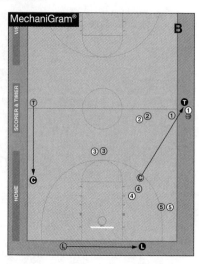

When a technical foul is called, the three officials should switch, just as they would with any foul. Technical foul free throws are administered in the same manner as other free throws: the lead administering the free throws, the center observing the free-thrower and the trail on or near the division line to observe the remaining nine players, as seen in MechaniGram A.

After all free throws have been attempted, the center will move up the court to the division line and administer the throw-in opposite the scorer's table, becoming the new trail. The trail will move down toward the endline to become the new center and the lead will move along the endline to balance the floor, as seen in MechaniGram B.

The calling official always has the option of going opposite if the situation is potentially heated.

Note: Non-shooting players do not have to be behind the division line

CREW OF THREE **CHAPTER** 13

SUBSTITUTIONS

- **HANDLING SUBSTITUTIONS** P. 138

HANDLING SUBTITUTIONS

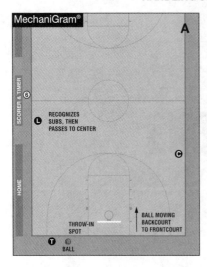
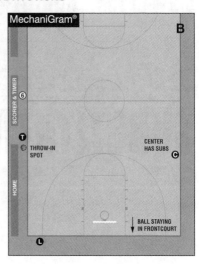

When substitutions are coming into the game, the official responsible depends on the location of the officials and where and how the ball will become live. During all substitutions, the responsible official should blow the whistle (if needed to get attention) and hold the "stop the clock" signal while beckoning substitutes.

• Throw-in with the ball staying in the frontcourt: In most situations, the official nearest the table is responsible.

• Throw-in with ball going from backcourt to frontcourt: If table side, the new lead recognizes the substitutes and then passes substitution responsibilities on to the center, as seen in MechaniGram A. If the new lead is opposite the table, the center has all substitution responsibilities.

• Prior to last free throw: The trail official has substitution responsibilities.

• Trail administering throw-in table side: The center has substitution responsibilities even though the center is across the court from the scorer's table as seen in MechaniGram B. The trail may not see the substitutes and the center has the best view of the scorer's table.

• Trail administering throw-in opposite the table: The center has substitution responsibilities.

The key to smooth substitutions is for all officials to have good communication, including eye contact.

2

CREW OF TWO

CREW OF TWO **CHAPTER** 14

TWO-PERSON PHILOSOPHY

Movement and compromise are the characteristics of two-person officiating. Ten players are moving around a closed court, competing for space and positions; two officials must utilize hustle, angles, distance and planned compromises to observe and control the action.

Hustle

Hustle is an overused word today. Everyone knows it's needed to succeed, but what does it really mean when relating it to two-person officiating? Think of it this way: NCAA conferences (from all Division I to most Division III conferences), plus the NBA use three officials per game. Many high school conferences and state tournaments are now using three officials. Why? Because of the speed, size, quickness and the physical nature of games at those levels, three officials can better control a game than two officials. That extra set of eyes and ears prevents many problems. Plus, athletic budgets allow it at those levels, something that would be difficult at the lower levels.

The game control expectations are no different with two officials, yet there's one less person to help control the game. Significant movement by both officials is critical for proper court coverage. Hustle gives you a chance. In essence, two officials must work hard enough to cover the entire court that is better covered by three officials. That equates to more running and a well-placed concern for angles.

Movements

Both officials must work hard at understanding, then obtaining, proper angles. Your line of sight must provide you with an opportunity to view a developing play or part of a play. You must be able to see completely through the play, which means your vision must be unobstructed by the players directly involved in the play and others near the play.

Basketball is a game of nearly continual motion. An official's angle and distance adjustments are constant as play is in motion. A step or two in the right direction may open up a whole new viewing experience, free from obstruction; a step in the wrong direction will screen you from the critical game action.

With two officials, the trail must move off (away from) the sideline for proper court coverage. Far too often officials who can't (or won't) run well stay on the sideline. They're afraid of getting in the way and aren't confident they can move quickly enough to avoid passing lanes and get good angles. The game suffers because court coverage suffers. A good trail official moves off the near sideline when the ball is nearer the far sideline; it's the best way to get good angles and proper distance from the play.

Why such an emphasis on trail movement? That allows the lead to watch players off-ball, the critical component to combating physical play. Rough play was a point of emphasis throughout the last decade. When the trail moves off the sideline to cover plays, the lead can focus on the lane area, where most rough play occurs.

The lead also moves along the endline to improve angles. There's usually at least four and sometimes six or eight players in the lane area battling for position. Lead movement is critical to watching low-post action. It's paramount to game control.

Proper movements on rebounding action are also important. Because there are only two officials, there's a tendency to think about moving to the other end of the court when a shot goes up to avoid getting beat downcourt. If either official ignores rebounding action, physical play develops and game control suffers. Both officials must move to get good angles on rebounding action.

Compromises

Two officials can't see everything. If they could, you'd see two officials in the Final Four and the NBA Finals. Though

all areas of officiating are important, conscious sacrifices must be made to ensure game control and quality off-ball officiating.

Because of the necessary emphasis on off-ball coverage, some boundary line coverage is compromised. It's simply a tradeoff. You're focusing on great off-ball coverage and giving up a bit of sideline coverage in some areas. You're playing the percentages because you're more likely to have rough play than you are to have close sideline violations that aren't obvious.

A complete understanding of court coverage

Proper coverage is enhanced by good eye contact and a "feel" for where your partner is looking. You must learn about all aspects of two-person officiating to know who is covering what. Once you've mastered that, practical on-court application develops through partner communication, including eye contact and understanding. At the risk of being obvious, you've got to know exactly what both you and your partner are expected to do in specific situations — then effectively communicate with your partner — to truly master two-person officiating. When you understand why angles and distance are important and how and when to obtain them, you'll find yourself in great position throughout each game.

CREW OF TWO **CHAPTER** 15

COURT POSITIONING

PREGAME

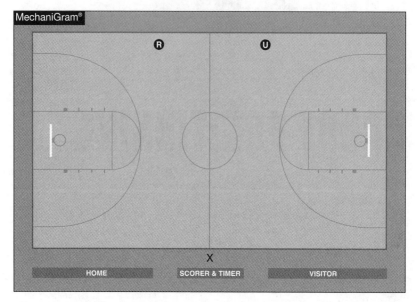

MechaniGram®

HOME   SCORER & TIMER   VISITOR

Arrive on the court at least 15 minutes prior to game time and position yourselves on the side of the court opposite the scorer's table. Each official should be approximately 28 feet from the nearest endline. The referee observes the visiting team warm-up, the umpire watches the home team.

During that time, officials should check the court area, markings and basket to make sure everything is legal and free from interference. Officials should also watch the teams warm-up to ensure no illegal activity occurs (dunking, etc.). Make yourself aware of player tendencies by watching the teams and players perform their pregame drills.

Referee recommendation: When the referee returns from the table after checking the scorebook, it might be advantageous for both officials to switch so that you can see each team during the warm-up period.

HALFTIME

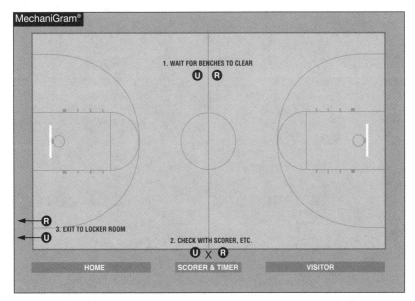

MechaniGram®

1. WAIT FOR BENCHES TO CLEAR

3. EXIT TO LOCKER ROOM

2. CHECK WITH SCORER, ETC.

HOME

SCORER & TIMER

VISITOR

At the conclusion of play for the first half, the officials are now positioned halfway between the farthest point of the center circle and the sideline opposite the scorer's table (1). After both teams have left their benches and gone to their respective locker rooms, both officials walk over to the scorer's table and the referee takes care of specified duties (2). After performing duties at the scorer's table, the officials leave together for their locker room. (3)

When the officials return to the court for the second half, the officials will stand across the court until the one-minute mark. At that time, the umpire will secure the ball and bounce it to the referee. The referee will take a position with the ball at the division line on the sideline opposite the table indicating the direction of play with the placement of the ball. The umpire shall take a position on the division line on the opposite edge of the restraining circle.

BETWEEN QUARTERS

MechaniGram®

HOME   SCORER & TIMER   VISITOR

During the intermission between quarters and any extra periods, the officials have specific spots on the floor. While holding the ball, the referee stands at the division line on the sideline opposite the table. The ball shall be placed on the side of the official that indicates the direction of play.

The umpire shall take a position on the division line on the opposite side edge of the restraining circle. The umpire is responsible for acknowledging substitutes and making sure that the report takes place prior to the warning signal.

There should be no visiting with coaches or players unless it is to confer about a game situation. The officials are then responsible to count the players when the teams return to the court to begin the play. Use preventive officiating to make sure there are five players active on the court per team.

CREW OF TWO

FULL TIMEOUT

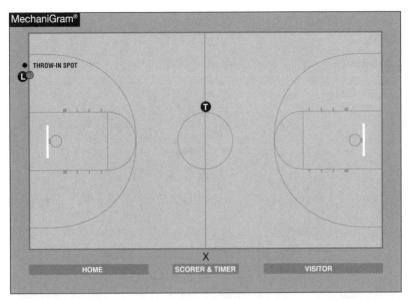

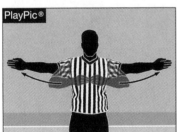

Wait until both teams have been able to get to their respective team benches before signaling for the timeout to begin.

During a 60-second timeout, the administering official should take the ball to where it will be put in play. If that official needs to leave the administering spot, he or she may place the ball on the floor at the spot. If play is to be resumed near the team benches, move out onto the floor to get away from the team. If play is resumed with a free throw, take a position on the free-throw line.

The non-administering official should be on the division line on the circle farthest from the table.

If activity on the court make it necessary to move, the officials should move to a safe location and move back to the designated spots at the conclusion of the activity.

At the first horn (45-second mark), the officials will step toward the nearest team huddle and notify the teams by raising and index finger and saying "first horn."

THIRTY-SECOND TIMEOUT

MechaniGram®

THROW-IN SPOT

L

T

X

HOME   SCORER & TIMER   VISITOR

PlayPic®
"Start the clock"

PlayPic®
"First horn"

Wait until both teams have been able to get to their respective team benches before signaling for the timeout to begin.

During a 30-second timeout, the administering official should take the ball to where it will be put in play. If that official needs to leave the administering spot, he or she may place the ball on the floor at the spot. If play is to be resumed near the team benches, move out onto the floor to get away from the team. If play is resumed with a free throw, take a position on the free-throw line.

The non-administering official should be on the division line on the circle closest to the table. That official is responsible for beckoning substitutes into the game and should be prepared to give the scorer or timer any necessary information.

If activity on the court make it necessary to move, the officials should move to a safe location and move back to the designated spots at the conclusion of the activity.

At the first horn (15-second mark), the officials will step toward the nearest team huddle and notify the teams by raising and index finger and saying "first horn."

CREW OF TWO

JUMP BALL

AFTER INTRODUCTIONS, BEFORE TIP-OFF

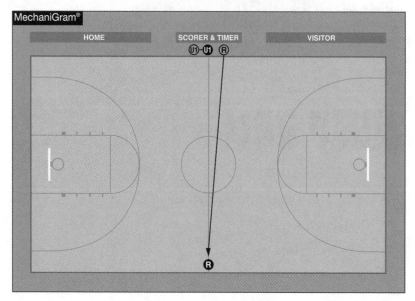

After the national anthem and the introductions of the players, the players are usually getting last words of instruction before going out onto the court. At that time, the officials should leave their positions at the scorer's table and go to specific locations on the court. The referee (or the official designated to throw the jump ball) takes the ball and moves to a spot near the far sideline, facing the scorer's table.

The umpire shall take a position on the table-side sideline, at the division line, facing the referee. That official should hustle the teams to get onto the court. Many times, teams will take an unnecessary amount of time with rituals or preparation. Get the teams on the court and ready to play.

Note: The referee can toss the jump ball or designate the umpire if that official throws a better jump ball. Within the book, the official tossing the ball will always be referred to as the referee.

POSITIONING

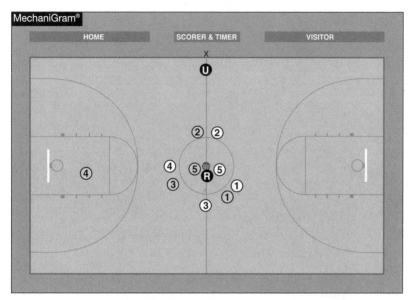

The umpire is positioned near the intersection of the sideline and the division line directly in front of the table. Before entering the center restraining circle, the referee makes eye contact with the umpire, who signals to the referee that table personnel and the umpire are ready to go. Both officials make sure the teams are facing the correct direction.

While still outside the circle, the referee notifies both team captains that play is about to begin. Tell the players to hold their spots to avoid violations. Blow the whistle with a sharp blast before entering the circle.

Before tossing the ball, you may want to use a bit of preventive officiating with the jumpers. Tell them to jump straight up and not into each other, and tell them not to tap the ball on the way up. Just before the toss, the umpire uses the "do not start clock" signal — raised open hand. The referee tosses the ball high enough so the players tap the ball on its downward flight. The umpire starts the clock when the ball is tapped.

The umpire must maintain a wide field of vision while the referee administers the toss. The umpire is primarily responsible for the position and action of the eight non-jumpers.

JUMP BALL GOES LEFT

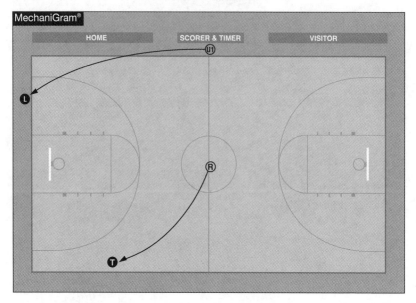

If the ball goes to the referee's left, U1 will move right and become the lead. The lead should be prepared to rule on a quick three-point attempt from anywhere on the court until the referee has cleared the players and begun to move into position.

The referee will hold momentarily and then will move to the trail enabling coverage of the sideline opposite the lead.

After the ball is possessed, the trail should glance at the alternating-possession arrow to make sure it is pointing in the right direction. If it isn't, wait for the first dead ball and correct it.

JUMP BALL GOES RIGHT

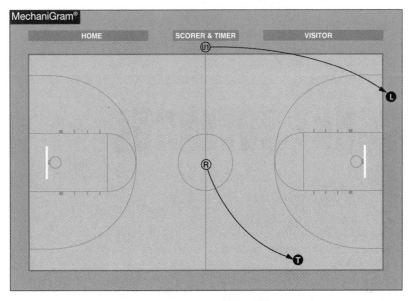

If the ball goes to the referee's right, U1 will move to the left and become the lead.

The referee will hold until players clear and then moves to become the trail. The referee will assume sideline responsibility opposite the lead.

After the ball is possessed, the trail should glance at the alternating-possession arrow to make sure it is pointing in the right direction. If it isn't, wait for the first dead ball and correct it.

Note: If possession is gained in the backcourt, the umpire may need to move with the ball to become the trail. If that happens, the referee would then move to the lead position.

CREW OF TWO **CHAPTER** 17

COURT COVERAGE

HALFCOURT BOUNDARY LINE

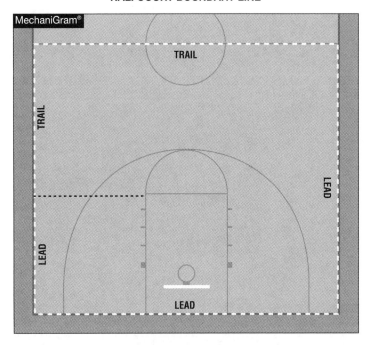

Covering boundary lines is among the most difficult tasks using a crew of two officials. By correctly placing so much emphasis on off-ball coverage for the lead, some boundary-line coverage sometimes gets sacrificed.

The NFHS manual states that in the frontcourt the lead is responsible for the sideline nearest the lead and the endline. The trail is responsible for the division line and the sideline nearest the trail. While in theory that sounds easy, the actual practice is very difficult and sacrifices off-ball coverage in the lane area.

Here's an example. A trouble spot for two-person crews is a player who has the ball near the sideline above the free-throw line extended and opposite the trail. The trail correctly moves toward the center of the court to officiate the action on the player with the ball, such as fouls, traveling violations, etc.

The problem: The manual states that sideline is the lead's responsibility. Well, if the lead has to look beyond the free-throw line extended to watch for a potential sideline violation and the trail has to watch for fouls, etc., who is watching the other players? No one. There are too many off-ball problems that can occur if no one is supervising those players.

Referee recommends that the trail also have opposite sideline responsibility above the free-throw line extended. Sometimes, the trail must move well beyond the center of the court to see an out-of-bounds violation. Stay deep (toward the division line) on the play to get a good angle.

Even with great hustle toward the far sideline, it is a tough look for the trail. The problem compounds if there's a swing pass back toward the other sideline. The trail must hustle back toward that sideline to get a good look there. Staying deep gives the trail a chance.

BOUNDARY COVERAGE: LEAD EXCEPTION

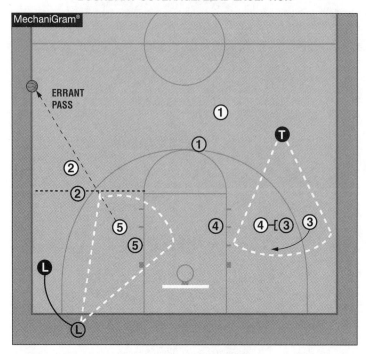

Though *Referee* recommends that the trail is responsible for the opposite sideline above the free-throw line extended, there is an exception.

When the floor is balanced, the lead is on-ball and a pass is thrown from the lane to a player above the free-throw line extended, the lead has initial responsibility of the entire sideline. Why? When the lead is on-ball, the trail is off-ball. The trail may not see an errant pass out-of-bounds above the free-throw line extended because the trail and lead haven't switched coverages yet. The trail can't effectively watch off-ball and see a quick pass made to the opposite sideline. The lead must help.

In the MechaniGram, team A has the ball in the low post. The lead is on-ball. The trail is correctly watching off-ball, including screening. While the trail is off-ball, team A throws an errant pass. The ball goes out-of-bounds above the free-throw line extended.

Since the lead was watching the play already and the trail was watching off-ball, the lead makes that call by moving toward the sideline and getting a good angle on the play. Though *Referee* suggests that would normally be the trail's call above the free-throw line extended, that coverage exception ensures quality off-ball coverage.

BASIC FRONTCOURT COVERAGE

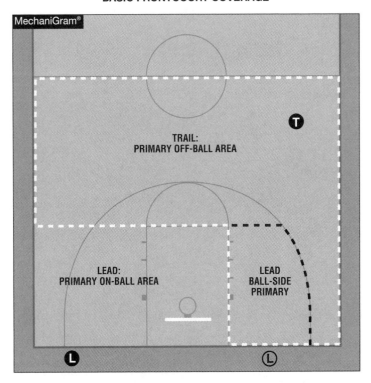

In the frontcourt, basic coverage shifts depending on which official is on-ball.

In the MechaniGram, the lead's on-ball responsibilities include the area below the free-throw line extended to the far edge of the free-throw lane line (away from the lead) when the lead is opposite the trail and the floor is balanced. If the lead is ball-side, the lead's area of responsibility grows. It includes the area below the free-throw line extended to the three-point arc.

When the lead is on-ball, the trail's off-ball responsibilities include the area above the free-throw line extended to the division line and the lane area from the free-throw lane line (nearest the trail) to the sideline nearest the trail. The trail's off-ball area of responsibility decreases when the lead is on-ball, ball-side. It is the area above the free-throw line extended and outside the three-point arc.

Officials are responsible for a five-second count within their primary coverage area. If the ball moves out of the official's primary area, that official should remain with that count until it is ended. Once the count has ended, return to your primary coverage area.

THREE-POINT RESPONSIBILITIES

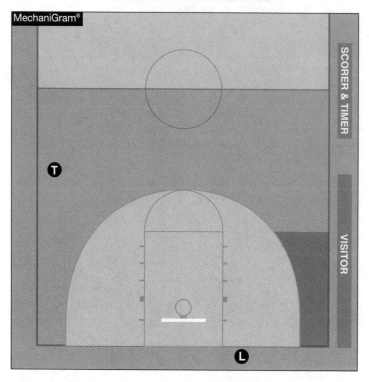

In the frontcourt, the trail is responsible for the majority of the three-point arc. The trail's coverage of a three-point try extends to the free-throw line extended opposite of the trail's current position. The lead is responsible for any attempt below the free-throw line extended on the lead's primary coverage area of the court.

On three-point trys, only the covering official should indicate the attempt. The indication should be made with the arm closest to the center of the court so the table personnel can see it better. Extend one arm above head level with three fingers extended. If successful, the covering official will signal by extending both arms over the head with palms facing.

If the trail official signals a successful three-point shot, the lead official shall not mirror the successful signal. If the lead official signals a successful three-point shot, the trail official mirrors the signal. There is no need to mirror an attempt signal.

The lead should be ready to assist the trail on a three-point attempt in transition.

HANDLING DOUBLE WHISTLES

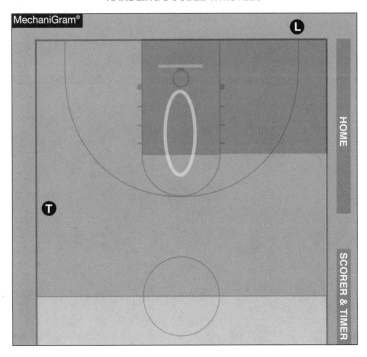

While coverage areas for all officials are well-defined, there can be areas on the court that occasionally are watched by more than one official.

There's a general rule for double whistles in a two-person system: Generally, the official who has primary coverage at the time of the whistles should take control of the call.

For example, if the dribbler is coming from the trail's primary area into the lead's area and there is a double whistle, the call is likely the trail's.

Another "trouble area" for double whistles occurs when a drive originates from the trail's primary area of coverage and ends up in the lane area, as seen in the MechaniGram. The reasoning: The ball originated in the trail's area so the trail stayed with the play and the lead picked up the penetrating player coming into the lane. There may be a brief moment in which both officials are watching the same area.

If the secondary official has a call that occurred before the primary official's call, the secondary official should close in quickly and take the call. An example might be a travel that occurs prior to a block/charge in the lane.

Double-whistles aren't the end of world. Sooner or later, they're going to happen. Just make sure when they do, they're not because of one official over-extending his or her coverage area. The keys:

1. Have good eye contact with your partner.
2. Understand where the play originated from.
3. Understand the primary area.
4. Allow the proper official to make the call.

Discuss double whistles during your pregame and how to handle.

SPLITTING COURT ON DRIVES

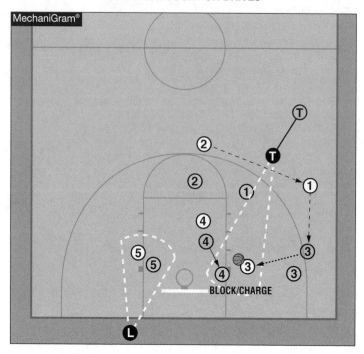

Sometimes, the lead doesn't have enough time to get ball side and get a good look on drives toward the basket. When players make quick passes away from the lead that cover a great distance, it's difficult to react in time to get a good angle.

When that happens, there's a simple solution: "You take the stuff on your side of the hoop and I'll take the stuff on my side of the hoop."

There's a great myth among referees that the lead is the only official who can call block/charge near the lane. That's wrong. That attitude places too much pressure on the lead because there's too much to watch. It also leaves the lead straightlined and guessing on many plays that aren't on the lead's side of the floor.

When the lead is on the far side of the court, the trail has a much better look on drives to the lane that start on the trail's half of the court. But it takes an aggressive, hard-working trail to make the call correctly and with conviction.

As the trail, penetrate toward the endline to get the proper angle on the drive to basket. Referee the defense. Make the call. It's really that simple.

In the MechaniGram, the officials start the play with the floor balanced. Team A throws a quick swing pass that player quickly drives to the basket. The action is too fast for the lead to move ball side. As the drive to the basket occurs, the secondary defender steps in to take a charge. The trail penetrates toward the endline, gets a good angle and makes the judgment on the contact.

Developing an aggressive mind-set as a trail official will help overall court coverage. Don't leave the lead alone. Do your part by taking the "stuff" on your side of the basket when the lead can't see clearly.

PASS/CRASH IN LANE

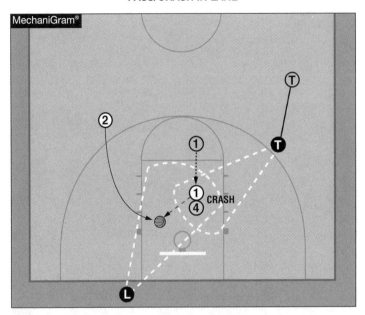

A player driving a crowded lane, passing off to a teammate, then crashing into a defender can be one of the most difficult plays to officiate. Why? There's a lot going on in a small area in a short period of time.

For the lead, the play is especially tough to handle alone. Did the passer get fouled? Did the passer foul? Block? Charge? Is it a team or player-control foul? Did the dribbler travel? Did the player filling the lane catch the pass cleanly and travel or did the player merely fumble and recover? Did the violation occur before the foul? That's way too much for one official to handle in most cases.

The trail must help. By aggressively penetrating toward the endline when players drive the lane, the trail can take some of the pressure off the lead by being in great position to judge the play.

The common phrase that sums up responsibilities is, "Lead takes the pass, trail takes the crash." That's generally accurate when the pass is toward the lead. However, when the pass is toward the trail (especially out toward the perimeter), the trail should take the pass and the lead take the crash.

The trail should watch the dribbler penetrate. Watch for the dribbler being fouled on the drive or while passing. Also, the trail watches for the dribbler crashing into a defender after releasing a pass that goes toward the lead. Referee the defense to see if the defender obtained legal guarding position. Be especially wary of dribblers who leave their feet to make a pass. Don't bail out an out-of-control player by making a no-call.

With the trail watching that action, the lead can concentrate primarily on the pass toward the lead and the player receiving it. Don't fall into the trap, however, of leaving all crashes to the trail. For the lead, the pass is primary, but the crash is secondary. You'd rather have a call on the crash from the lead than a no-call that lets a foul get away. Make a call as the lead if you have to.

REBOUNDING AREAS

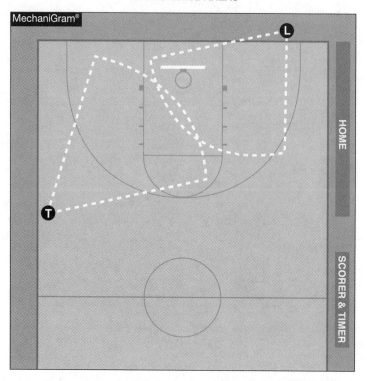

Rebounding coverages are divided and fall into primary and secondary coverage areas. If a shot is taken near the trail, the trail has to make sure the shooter returns to the floor without contact and then must watch the ball to determine for any violations. It's imperative to also watch the rebounding action on that side of the court. The lead will watch on his or her side of the court and extend that coverage into the lane area.

In a two-person crew, getting fouls on rebounds is all about obtaining the proper angle on the play. Many times, the trail official will have the best opportunity to determine a shove in the back. The lead might be closer but not able to see through so many players in a congested area.

CREW OF TWO

OFFICIATING THE DELAY OFFENSE

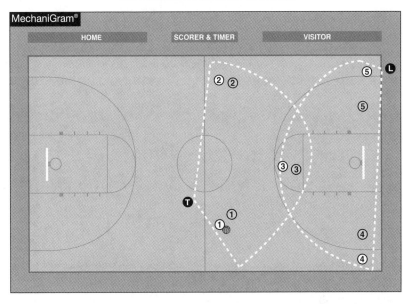

The delay offense, sometimes referred to as the "spread," presents unique challenges for officiating crews. The delay offense spreads players out to all corners of the frontcourt and is designed to run the clock down while avoiding double teams.

When a team goes into a delay offense, the wing officials may have to referee from outside the court, as seen in the MechaniGram, to keep wide triangle coverage. That way, the players have enough room to maneuver without using you as a screen. It also keeps you out of the passing lanes.

BACKCOURT BOUNDARY

In the backcourt, the new trail is responsible for the backcourt endline and the sideline opposite the new lead. The new lead is responsible for the frontcourt endline. That's the easy part. Who's got the sideline opposite the new trail and who's got the division line?

The sideline opposite the trail in the backcourt is a shared responsibility. Simply stated, when the new lead is looking in the area where the sideline violation occurs, the new lead makes the call. Actual practice can be a bit of a challenge though.

Proper coverage is necessitated by good eye contact and a "feel" for where the new lead is looking. One general rule of thumb: If you were on-ball immediately before a play near the sideline, you've likely got sideline responsibility. (One notable exception is when the new lead is helping with backcourt pressure, is positioned on the sideline and the ball goes out-of-bounds near the new lead. It would be odd to have the new trail make an out-of-bounds call from an appreciable distance when the ball went out-of-bounds in close proximity to the new lead.)

If the new lead is already looking in the area (on-ball or off-ball) where the out-of-bounds violation occurs, the new lead can make that call. If the new lead is running into the frontcourt watching players in transition (off-ball) and the play happens behind the new lead, the new trail has sideline responsibility.

Help each other out. If the new lead whistles an out-of-bounds violation on the new lead's sideline but doesn't know who caused the violation, blow the whistle, stop the clock and look for help from the new trail.

With a transition play near the division line, the new lead has initial responsibility until the new trail is in position to get a good look at the division line. Eye contact and a feel for where your partner is watching play an important role in who has division line responsibility.

BACKCOURT NO PRESSURE

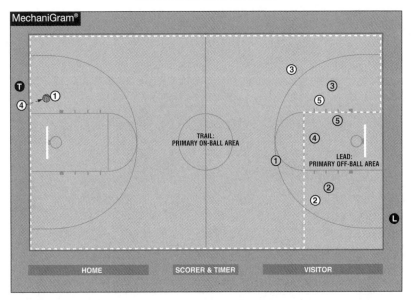

When play moves from one endline toward the other, the trail has primary responsibility in the backcourt. For example, after a made basket the trail is responsible for the throw-in and watches the players move to the other end of the court.

In any transition effective coverage means significant movement by the trail. Similar to halfcourt coverage, the trail must move off the sideline. The trail must stay behind the players as the ball is being brought up the court.

CREW OF TWO

BACKCOURT WITH PRESSURE

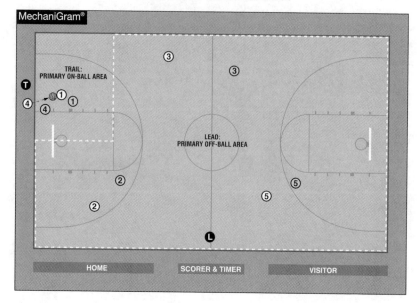

When play moves from one endline toward the other, the trail has primary responsibility in the backcourt. However, when there's defensive pressure in the backcourt, sometimes the lead must help.

There is a general rule when the lead helps the trail in the backcourt. If there are four or fewer players in the backcourt, the trail works alone there. More than four players, the lead helps.

When there's more than four players in the backcourt, the lead is positioned near the division line. If all the players are in the backcourt, the lead may move closer to the backcourt endline for better angles. If some players are in the frontcourt, however, the division-line area is the best position.

When near the division line, the lead must stay wide and constantly glance from backcourt to frontcourt. That "swivel" glance allows the lead to help the trail with backcourt traffic plus watch players in the frontcourt.

The lead should be ready to help on out-of-bounds calls, long passes and possible infractions involving the division line. The lead will also cover quick breaks and long passes, keeping the players boxed in.

LAST-SECOND SHOT

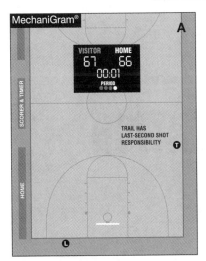

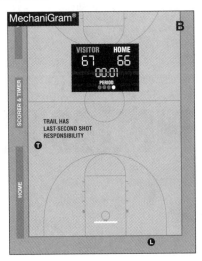

The trail official is responsible for making the call on any last-second shot and should communicate that with his or her partner. It doesn't matter what side of the court the shot is attempted from, the call will always be made by the trail.

When the ball is inbounded in the backcourt and a long pass is expected, the lead should be prepared to assist. If the non-responsible official has information regarding the allowing or disallowing of a basket to share with the calling official, he or she should go directly to the responsible official for a brief discussion. The referee will make the final decision in the case of disagreement or if it is necessary to consult the timer. Use timeouts near the end of any period to communicate the coverage for any last-second shot.

CREW OF TWO **CHAPTER** 18

THE LEAD POSITION

BALL-SIDE MECHANICS

The lead must anticipate the play (that does not mean anticipate a foul) and move across the endline to get an angle on the action moving toward the open spot. In the MechaniGram above, the lead official has moved across the endline to clearly see the post player catch the ball and attempt a shot. The lead's in a great position to see the oncoming defensive players and any potential violations or fouls. Generally, the lead will only move ball side when the perimeter player with the ball is near or below the free-throw line extended.

Keep your head and shoulders turned toward the players in the lane when moving. Remember, you still have responsibilities for watching the screen and other action in your primary area. If you put your head down and sprint across the lane to the new spot, you will miss off-ball contact. Move with dispatch, but move under control and with your eyes on your primary off-ball area. If the ball moves out of the post area, simply move back to your original position to balance the floor with the trail.

The lead moves for two reasons: The lead is in a better position to see the play clearly (if the lead stayed on the off-ball side he would be looking through bodies and guessing) and the lead is closer to the play, which helps sell the call or no-call. Perception is important. If you look like you're close to the play and in good position, your ruling has a better chance of being accepted.

MOVEMENT AFTER BASKET

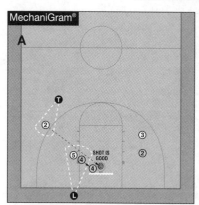

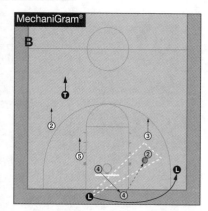

When the lead is ball side watching action in the post and a goal is scored, there's no need to rush back to the lane line opposite the trail and balance the floor. If immediately after the made basket you can balance the floor without interfering with the ensuing play and without missing action around the throw-in area, do so.

However, in most situations there is not enough time to balance the floor without interfering and missing action. If you don't have time to get over, don't panic. You've still got a pretty good angle to watch all the action.

Watch for players interfering with the ball after the made basket. Watch the player collect the ball and move out-of-bounds for the throw-in. Then, watch the thrower, the throw-in and action in the lane area. You can do all that from the lane line on the trail side of the floor.

After the throw-in is made, quickly swing behind the thrower toward the far sideline to balance the floor.

In MechaniGram A, the lead is ball side watching the post players when team A makes a jump shot. Team B grabs the ball and moves out-of-bounds for a throw-in. The lead does not have enough time to balance the floor before the throw-in. In MechaniGram B, team B is out-of-bounds and throws a quick inbounds pass. The lead, still on the opposite side, watches the thrower and throw-in, then quickly swings behind the thrower to balance the floor.

MOVEMENT TOWARD SIDELINE

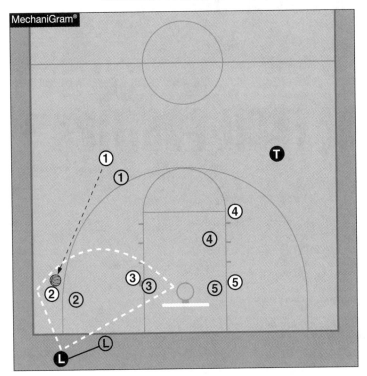

When the ball drops below the free-throw line extended on the lead side of the court, the lead has two responsibilities: Watch the post players on the near low block and watch the perimeter player with the ball. It is difficult to see both areas.

To give yourself a chance, back off the endline and move toward the sideline. Your shoulders should not be parallel to the endline. Angle them slightly; that movement increases your field of vision and gives you a chance to see both areas.

Primary coverage is on-ball; secondary coverage is off-ball. With that improved position, the lead has a chance to see both in his field of view.

CREW OF TWO **CHAPTER** 19

THE TRAIL POSITION

- INSIDE-OUT LOOK P. 173

- MOVEMENT OFF SIDELINE P. 174

- MOVEMENT ON JUMP SHOT P. 175

- TRAIL PICKS UP SHOOTER P. 176

- TRAIL WORKS BACKSIDE P. 177

- TRAIL LOOKS WEAK SIDE P. 178

INSIDE-OUT LOOK

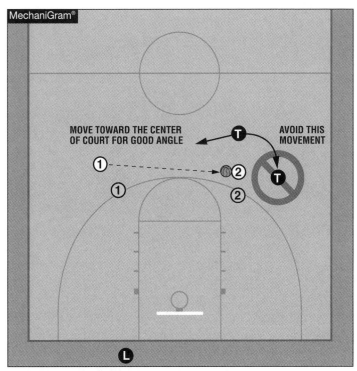

MechaniGram®

MOVE TOWARD THE CENTER OF COURT FOR GOOD ANGLE

AVOID THIS MOVEMENT

With a crew of two officials, the trail official often has to get off the sideline and move toward the center of the court to officiate action on the far side of the floor. When that happens, the trail can get caught in the middle on a swing pass from one side of the court to the other. Adjustments must be made.

When a swing pass moves from the sideline opposite the trail across the top of the key to the near-side wing, the trail can get straightlined because of the position off the sideline. When a quick swing pass straightlines you and gives you a poor angle, you must make an adjustment to improve the angle.

A simple one- or two-step adjustment toward the center of the court gives you the proper angle. You must fight the urge to run around the entire play toward the sideline, using six steps or more and wasting precious time. By the time you run around the play, the offensive player could take a shot (was the shooter's foot on or behind the three-point arc?), violate or be fouled — and you may not have seen it.

After adjusting one or two steps toward the center to improve your angle, watch the entire play from there, including a jump shot follow-through and landing. After you've taken care of that responsibility, you can move toward the sideline and endline, working for your next good angle on rebounding action.

CREW OF TWO

MOVEMENT OFF SIDELINE

MechaniGram®

Effective court coverage requires significant movement by the trail.

When an offensive player has the ball on the side of the floor opposite the trail, the trail must move away from the near sideline and get proper angles. By staying too close to the near sideline, the trail cannot effectively see action near the ball and must make judgments from a distance — way too far away to convince anyone the trail saw the play correctly.

In the MechaniGram, the player with the ball is far away from the trail official — though the player is still the trail's responsibility — and there's defensive pressure. To see the play well, the trail must move off the near sideline and work to get a good angle.

Avoid moving straight toward the play: You could interfere with the play by stepping into a passing lane. Take an angle toward the division line to decrease your chances of interfering with the play. In extreme cases, you may even position yourself in the backcourt.

By moving off the sideline and angling toward the backcourt, you're in a much better position to see the play.

MOVEMENT ON JUMP SHOT

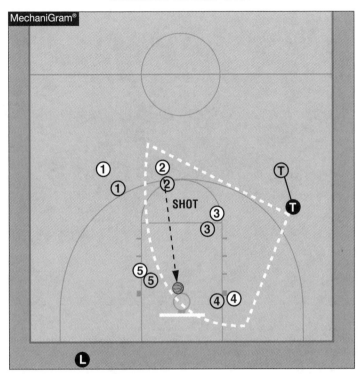

The trail has more responsibilities than simply watching the shooter. Too often a shot goes up and the trail's first thought is to start moving to the other end of the floor to avoid getting beat down court. When the trail leaves, the lead is left with offensive players crashing the boards and defensive players doing all they can to grab the rebound. That's too much for one person to handle.

The trail must help with rebounding action. When a player takes a jump shot within the trail's coverage area, the first responsibility is to watch the airborne shooter all the way back to the floor to ensure there are no offensive or defensive fouls. While watching that action, the trail should be moving a couple of steps toward the endline.

Once everything is OK with the shooter and surrounding action, the steps toward the endline allow the trail to help the lead by watching rebounding action. A step or two to improve your angle is all that's necessary to successfully watch rebounding action. Avoid going below the free-throw line extended. The trail is likely to see an offensive player pushing (or crashing into) a defensive player from behind — something that is difficult for the lead to see from the endline.

Do the game, your partner and yourself a favor and resist the urge to sprint to the other end of the floor when the shot goes up. Move toward the endline to get rebounding angles.

TRAIL PICKS UP SHOOTER

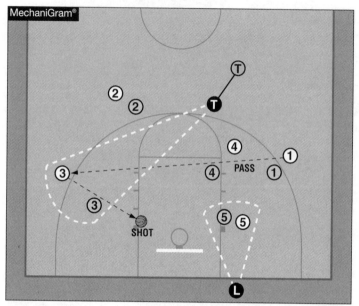

In two-person mechanics, the lead official should move to the ball side of the lane when the player with the ball is below the free-throw line extended and a potential post pass is evident.

Though ball-side mechanics are effective for controlling post play, one weakness is coverage of a skip pass to the opposite wing player for a quick shot. A skip pass is a quick pass from one side of the floor to the other, designed to take advantage of a sagging defense. Taboo years ago, it's now seen at virtually every level.

Though the opposite wing player is primarily observed by the lead official (even though the lead moved ball side), when a skip pass occurs the trail should adjust a step or two toward the wing player (to the center of the floor) and get a good angle to rule on three-point attempts, fouls and possibly obvious out-of-bounds infractions. Though a long-distance look, that's better than having the lead guess because the lead's looking through lane traffic or sprinting head-down to the other side of the court and missing the banging going on in the post.

If there is no quick shot and the lead can adjust back to the other side of the court without haste, the lead then picks up the ball (assuming it is below the free-throw line extended) and the trail moves back toward the sideline, getting good angles to watch off-ball. The lead must continue to watch off-ball in the lane area while moving until completely across the lane and in a good position to pick up the player with the ball.

In the MechaniGram, the lead has moved ball side when a skip pass is thrown and that player immediately shoots. Since the lead is ball side and doesn't have enough time to balance the floor, the trail picks up the shot, even though the attempt is below the free-throw line extended. The trail should penetrate slightly toward the play to improve the angle.

A good pregame conference and good eye contact during the game give you a better chance to officiate the skip pass correctly.

TRAIL WORKS BACKSIDE

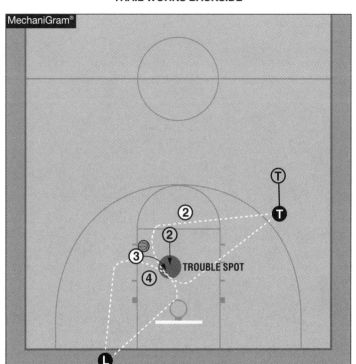

A trouble spot for the lead develops when a player with the ball on the low block spins toward the middle of the lane away from the lead. The quick spin move often leaves the lead straightlined and without a good look on the play.

Many times, a defender near the free-throw line will drop down into the lane and challenge the move toward the basket. That's when you'll likely see that defender slap at the offensive player, trying to poke the ball away. That steal attempt is sometimes a foul — one that goes unseen by the now-straightlined lead.

The trail must help out and watch the area in the lane when a post player spins away from the lead. Commonly referred to as the lead's "backside," the trail has a much better look at the play after penetrating toward the endline for an improved angle.

In the MechaniGram, the post player has the ball on the low block in front of the lead. That player spins toward the middle of the lane and drives toward the basket. The defender drops down and attempts the steal. The lead watches the post up action and the initial spin move. The trail penetrates toward the endline, gets a good angle and watches the perimeter defender on the play. The lead's backside is protected.

Come in strong and sell the call if you're the trail and you see a foul. Move toward the call to cut down the distance on the play. Perception is important. If you look like you're close to the play and in good position your ruling has a better chance of being accepted.

TRAIL LOOKS WEAK SIDE

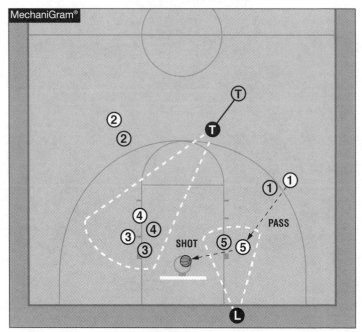

There are many benefits of the lead moving ball side for post action. One potential problem, however, is weak-side rebounding action. With the lead on the same side of the floor as the trail, the lane area opposite both officials can present problems.

With the lead ball-side and already watching post play near the closest lane line, it is difficult for the lead to watch players away from that area in the lane. First, primary concentration is — and should be — on the post play. Second, it is difficult for the lead to see the opposite side of the lane because the lead is looking through lane congestion and is easily straightlined.

When the lead moves ball side, it is the trail's responsibility to observe weak-side rebounding action. Though somewhat of a long-distance look, with the proper penetration toward the endline to get a good angle the trail can effectively watch weak-side rebounding action.

In the MechaniGram, the trail watches the perimeter player deliver a drop pass to the post player, who has effectively posted up on the low block. The lead already moved ball side anticipating the play. The post player seals off the defender and pivots strongly to the basket. The lead watches the post-up action.

Anticipating the play, the trail adjusts for a good angle and looks opposite. From that spot, the trail can look through the lane and watch the players battle on the weak side for rebounding positioning.

If you're the trail and you see a foul on the weak side, penetrate toward the lane and sell the call. By moving into the lane area aggressively (roughly around the intersection of the lane line and the free-throw line), the trail will cut the distance. Perception is important. If you look like you're close to the play and in good position, your ruling has a better chance of being accepted.

CREW OF TWO **CHAPTER** 20

TRANSITIONS

- **BUMP AND RUN** P. 180

- **TRAIL MOVEMENT OFF SIDELINE** P. 181

- **LEAD HELPS IN BACKCOURT** P. 182

- **PASS/CRASH IN TRANSITION** P. 183

- **LEAD HELPS ON THREE POINTER** P. 184

- **THE BUTTON HOOK** P. 185

BUMP AND RUN

MechaniGram®

DRIBBLER CAUSES BALL
TO GO OUT-OF-BOUNDS

HOME   SCORER & TIMER   VISITOR

The bump-and-run is a mechanic used by two-person crews to move swiftly from the frontcourt after a violation.

As the trail official, when an offensive violation occurs in your coverage area, stop the clock, signal the violation and the direction, then point to the spot for the throw-in. Next — after checking that there are no problems — sprint down court while viewing the action behind you and become the new lead official.

If you're the lead, eye the trail's signals, move toward the spot for the throw-in and administer it. You have now become the new trail. The lead "bumps" the trail down court and the trail moving to lead "runs" the floor.

In the MechaniGram, team A causes the ball to go out-of-bounds. The trail correctly stops the clock, signals a violation and the direction, then communicates the throw-in spot to the lead. The trail then moves down court and becomes the new lead.

On occasion, the trail may cut across the court when moving to lead. It saves time and allows your partner to put the ball in play quickly. Be careful, however; the trail-to-lead movement should not cut across the court if players are quickly moving downcourt because a collision may occur. Whether you remain near the sideline or cut across the court, the new lead's field of vision must keep players in sight — looking for potential problems — while moving down court. The new lead must balance the court on the throw-in and assume responsibility for the sideline opposite the throw-in.

The bump-and-run serves two main purposes: The trail official has a better chance of avoiding problems near the violation and the officials move into place quicker and get the ball live faster. Also, the bump-and-run gets the ball live faster.

CREW OF TWO

THE MOVEMENT OFF SIDELINE

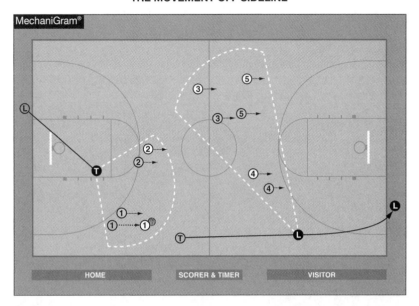

Effective two-person court coverage requires significant movement by the trail off the sideline. The same philosophies are true in the transition game when play is moving from the backcourt to the frontcourt.

When an offensive player has the ball on the side of the floor opposite the trail, the trail must move away from the near sideline and get proper angles. By staying too close to the near sideline, the trail cannot effectively see action near the ball and must make judgments from a distance — way too far to convince anyone the trail saw the play correctly.

In the MechaniGram, the offense dribbles the ball upcourt opposite the new trail as defensive pressure is applied. The rest of the players are advancing to the frontcourt as the new lead watches off-ball. To see the play well, the new trail must move far off the near sideline and work to get a good angle.

Stay deep. Avoid moving straight toward the play because you could interfere with the play by stepping into a passing lane. Take an angle toward the backcourt endline to decrease your chances of interfering with the play.

By moving off the sideline and angling toward the play, you're in a much better position to see the play.

LEAD HELPS IN BACKCOURT

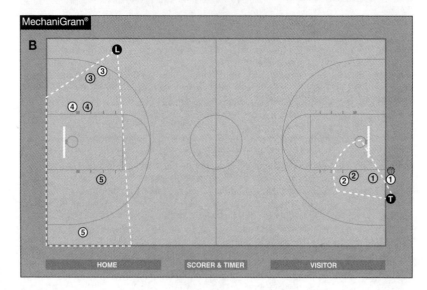

In MechaniGram A, there are six players in the backcourt. The lead is positioned near the division line to help with backcourt players away from the trail. The lead must also watch players in the frontcourt.

In MechaniGram B, there are four players in the backcourt. The trail is responsible for all of those players. The lead moves into the frontcourt and watches all players there, eventually moving to the frontcourt endline.

PASS/CRASH IN TRANSITION

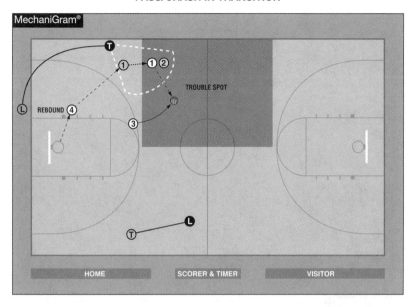

The same pass/crash principles that apply in the lane area apply all over the court. One trouble spot for officials is the pass/crash when a team in transition starts a break up the court. Many times you'll see players leave their feet to make a pass then crash into defenders. Block? Charge? No-call?

In the MechaniGram, the rebounder throws an outlet pass to a streaking teammate. That player catches the pass and dribbles up court trying to start a fastbreak.

The defender steps in to stop the offensive player from advancing into the frontcourt. As the offensive player leaps into the air and passes to a teammate, a crash ensues.

The lead must quickly read the fastbreak and move toward the sideline to become the new trail. The new trail has a good look at the offensive player leaping, passing and crashing.

The trail who becomes the new lead must also quickly read the fastbreak and move into the frontcourt. The new lead's primary responsibility is the player catching the pass. In rare circumstances, if the new trail did not get out on the break fast enough to see the crash, the new lead's secondary coverage area is the crash. That is more likely, however, when the pass/crash occurs in the center of the court.

LEAD HELPS ON THREE-POINTER

The transition game is difficult to cover with a crew of two officials. It's especially tough when quick outlet passes lead to quick shots at the other end of the court.

When quick, long passes advance the ball upcourt, the new lead must be prepared to help the trail determine whether or not a shot is a three-point try. The help occurs even though the shot attempt is in an area not normally covered by the lead. Why help? When there's a quick outlet pass that leads to another quick, long pass, the new trail usually doesn't have enough time to get into the frontcourt and get a good angle on a shot. Because of the distance and poor angle between the trail and the shot, the trail is left guessing.

The new lead must recognize the quick transition play and help the new trail by judging the shot.

In the MechaniGram, the rebounder throws a quick, long outlet pass to a teammate, who throws another quick, long pass to another teammate. That player catches the pass near the center restraining circle, dribbles to the top of the key and shoots. The lead moving to new trail doesn't have enough time to get a good look at the shot. The trail moving to new lead recognizes that and makes the judgment on the shot, even though a top-of-the-key shot is normally covered by the trail.

When that type of transition play occurs near the end of a period, the new lead judges whether or not the shot was a three-pointer, but the trail still judges whether the shot was released in time — unless alternate coverage was previously discussed.

THE BUTTON HOOK

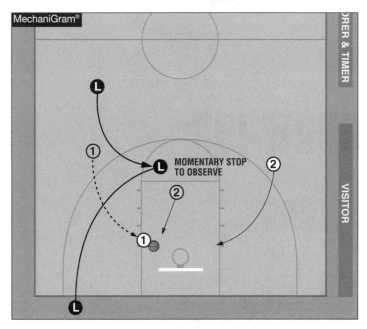

There are times when officials get beat downcourt on fastbreaks, especially in two-person. That's OK. In fact, if you're so worried about not getting beat you're probably leaving the lead official hanging alone with all the rebounding action — a definite no-no.

When you do get beat downcourt, there's no need to panic. There's a simple movement — the button hook — that can eliminate straightlining and allow you to officiate the play properly from behind. (It's called the button hook because the movement is similar to a football wide receiver's movement on a button hook pass pattern.)

Too often, an official who is trailing a fastbreak sprints as fast as possible (sometimes with their heads down) to stay even with the players. Staying even with the players is about the worst thing you can do for your angles. Either get ahead of the play and let it come comfortably to you (unlikely, unless you're a world-class sprinter) or let it go and momentarily officiate the play from behind. Staying even means you're looking through bodies and guessing.

When officiating a play from behind, swing toward the middle of the court, roughly at the intersection of the lane line and the free-throw line. Momentarily pause there to watch the action (referee the defense). That movement allows you a good angle to observe potential contact. When that part of the play is over, swing back out toward the sideline and endline to get into proper position.

Be aware of players coming from behind you. You should be well ahead of the second wave of players coming down court. They'll see you in the middle of the court and avoid contact. Make sure your position in the center of the court is momentary; you want to move out of there before the second wave comes down. If you feel pressure from players behind you, think safety first.

The button hook is a quick, simple movement that will eliminate the guesswork when trailing a play. It will help you get good angles.

CREW OF TWO **CHAPTER** 21

THROW-INS

BOXING IN: LEAD ADMINISTERS

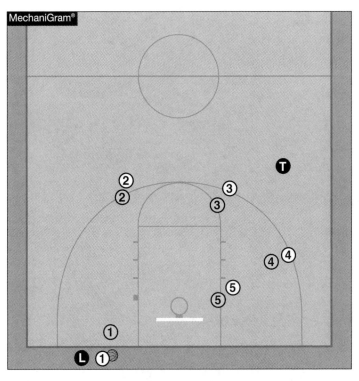

The lead administers all throw-ins on the frontcourt endline. All throw-ins shall be made from outside the thrower between the sideline and the thrower. The trail is positioned between the free-throw line extended and the division line, opposite the lead, to ensure both sidelines, both endlines and the division line are covered. The trail is also responsible for mirroring the chop of the lead.

The lead should always hand the ball to the thrower when remaining in the frontcourt.

BOXING IN: TRAIL ADMINISTERS

MechaniGram®

When the trail administers the throw-in, the thrower is always between the trail and the frontcourt basket. Unless otherwise dictated by an anticipated play, the lead is positioned on the endline opposite the trail to ensure both sidelines, the frontcourt endline and the division line are covered.

There are two ways the officials might have wound up in the positions shown in the MechaniGram. Under NFHS mechanics, the old lead would have been responsible for out-of-bounds calls along the sideline where the ball went out. Since the ball is being taken out above the free-throw line extended, the lead would move up the sideline to new trail, while the trail would move to new lead.

Referee recommendation: The officials will switch sides of the court, trail continuing in the trail position, lead continuing in the lead position. That makes it consistent that the only time a switch in the halfcourt happens is on a foul. It's simply a move from one side of the court to the other for the trail to handle the throw-in.

Make sure you discuss those options in the pregame discussion with your partner.

LEAD BALL SIDE

When the trail administers the throw-in, the thrower is always between the trail and the frontcourt basket. Normally, the lead is opposite the trail, however the players' location on the court now dictates the lead to be ball-side for the throw-in, while taking a position on the endline.

Even though the lead is ball-side, the lead is still responsible for two boundary lines: the endline and sideline opposite the trail. The lead is making a conscience decision to be ball-side, sacrificing the lead's sideline coverage for superior off-ball coverage.

If the lead were to balance the court by staying opposite the trail, the lead would be too far away from the players to officiate properly. Go where you need to in order to see the play but help out the trail so that he or she doesn't have to officiate the throw-in and all 10 players. Remember, perception is reality and the closer you are to the action, the easier it is to sell your call.

BOXING IN: TRAIL IN BACKCOURT

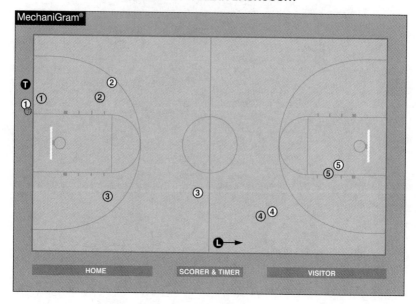

The trail administers all throw-ins in the backcourt. The thrower is always between the trail and the thrower's goal. Depending on backcourt pressure, the lead is positioned near the division line on the sideline opposite the trail, to ensure both sidelines and both endlines are covered.

The trail should bounce the ball to the thrower in the backcourt, unless there is defensive pressure.

THROW-IN ABOVE FREE THROW LINE

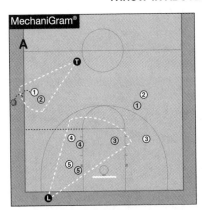

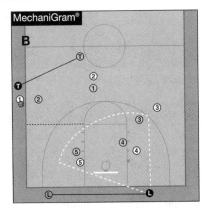

The NFHS manual states, "The throw-in is administered by the official responsible for the boundary line." The trail administers all throw-ins that occur above the free-throw line extended on either side of the floor so the lead can watch off-ball.

In MechaniGram A, the ball is knocked out of bounds by the defender along the trail's sideline and primary coverage area.

In MechaniGram B, the trail administers the throw-in above the free-throw line extended and assumes all responsibility for starting (chopping) the clock. The trail can bounce the ball to the thrower and back up as necessary. The lead will be responsible for off-ball coverage. Both officials should be alert for timeout requests.

THROW-IN BELOW FREE THROW LINE

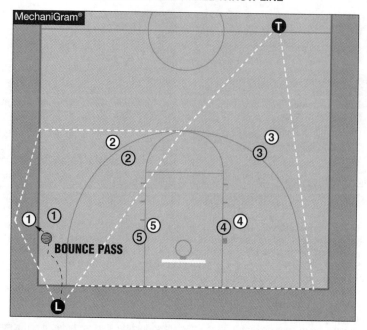

The lead has primary on-ball coverage when the ball is below the free-throw line extended opposite the trail. When a throw-in occurs on the sideline opposite the trail below the free-throw line extended, the lead administers the throw-in using the boxing-in method by bouncing the ball to the thrower.

The adjustments means the lead and trail will not have to switch or move across the court to administer a throw-in below the free-throw line extended, a necessary practice in previous seasons.

In order for the lead to administer the sideline throw-in, significant coverage adjustments must be made. The lead must move closer toward the sideline before bouncing the ball to the thrower to ensure a proper visual field that includes the thrower and throw-in plane. The lead should also get deep (move back away from the endline) to increase the field of vision and see secondary coverage of post play on the low block (MechaniGram).

With the lead focused nearer the throw-in, the trail must move off the opposite sideline and onto the court to officiate all off-ball action, including action in the lane area. The trail must be aggressive if an off-ball foul in the lane is detected, moving toward the foul to close the distance. The trail is also responsible for mirroring the chop of the lead.

As with all throw-ins, the lead and trail should make eye contact before the lead bounces the ball to the thrower.

Keep in mind the lead administers throw-ins below the free-throw line extended when the ball goes out of bounds on the lead's side of the court. If the ball goes out of bounds below the free-throw line extended on the trail's side of the court (opposite the lead), the trail administers that throw-in. There's no need for the lead to come across the court to administer that throw-in because the trail would also have to cross the court to apply boxing-in principles.

AFTER BACKCOURT VIOLATION

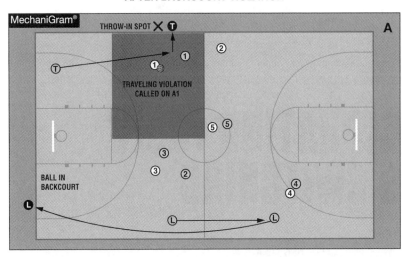

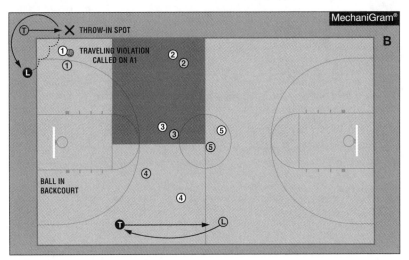

If a violation or out-of-bounds situation occurs in a team's backcourt and reverses the direction of play so that the throw-in team is in the frontcourt, the ball will be inbounded by the official responsible for that boundary line. The change will take place only if the violation or out-of-bounds situation occurs on the trail's half of the court in the area between the free-throw line extended and division line as shown.

In MechaniGram A, a traveling violation has been whistled on A1 in the backcourt between the free-throw line extended and division line. As shown in MechaniGram B, the trail official will stay and put the ball in play going the opposite direction for team B, becoming the "new trail." The previous lead will swing down the court and become the "new lead" on the opposite end.

CREW OF TWO **CHAPTER** 22

REPORTING FOULS & SWITCHING

FOUL REPORTING AREA

MechaniGram®

SCORER & TIMER

HOME

FOUL REPORTING AREA

Being a good dead-ball official means a variety of things, including watching players and reporting and signaling effectively during a dead ball. When a foul is called, you must fight the instinct to mentally relax because you think the action has stopped. Playing action may have stopped, but your dead-ball duties and responsibilities have just begun. The impact of your dead-ball officiating will affect live ball game action.

In the MechaniGram, the lead official has called a foul on the defender in the low post. At that time, the lead must do a number of things:

1. Delay momentarily after signaling the foul at the spot to ensure there is no continuing action or trash-talk among the players.

2. Do not worry about the basketball. Many times the ball will bounce away from the area. It is not your responsibility to chase it! Going after the ball leaves players unattended.

3. Once the immediate area appears calm, the lead clears all the players by running around them toward the reporting area. Do not run through a crowd because then players are behind you and you lose sight of them. That's when problems occur. Plus, by running around the crowd, you're ensuring your safety and their safety; you don't want any accidental bumps or trips to hurt anyone.

4. Stop and square up to the scorer's table in the reporting area. Make eye contact with the scorer before communicating and do not get too close to the table. If you run too close to the table, you're losing sight of bench conduct and you're giving the coaches an easier chance to voice displeasure with the call.

5. Give clear, crisp signals. Make sure most everyone sees what you called.

SWITCHING ON FOULS: NO FREE THROWS

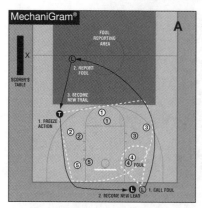

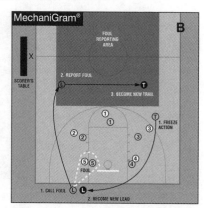

Officials switch positions on all non-shooting fouls, regardless of backcourt or frontcourt.

For shooting fouls, the calling official reports the foul to the table, then remains table side at trail. The calling official has the option of going to lead (opposite table) to avoid a confrontational situation with a coach/bench after a technical foul or disqualifying foul.

In MechaniGram A, the lead opposite the table has called a foul in the post that will result in an out-of-bounds throw-in. The lead will report the foul and switch with the trail table side. The table-side trail will move to become the new lead opposite the table and handle the ensuing throw-in. The non-calling official should force the switch just prior to the ball being brought back into play and get the players lined up for the throw-in.

In MechaniGram B, the lead table side has called a foul in the post. The lead will move to the foul reporting area to report the foul and then proceed to the trail position opposite the table. The old trail will move to the table-side lead position and handle the ensuing throw-in.

SWITCHING ON FOULS: LEAD CALL WITH FREE THROWS

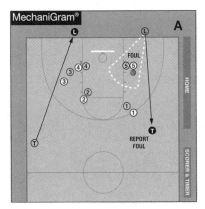

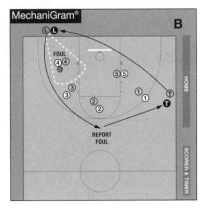

In free-throw situations (shooting or bonus), the rotations will vary depending upon your spot on the court. The calling official will always assume the table-side trail position for all free throws.

In MechaniGram A, the table-side lead official calls a foul on the low block that will result in free throws. The lead will report the foul and then assume the new table-side trail position. While the lead has switched positions, he or she will stay on the same side of the court. The trail opposite the table will freeze and then move to the lead position opposite the table to administer the free throws. Get the players lined up while your partner reports the foul and then confirm the number of attempts with your partner prior to bouncing the ball to the shooter.

In MechaniGram B, the lead official opposite the table has whistled a shooting foul. The lead will move to report the foul and then assume the table-side trail position. The old table-side trail will move to the new lead position opposite the table to administer the free throws. That scenario will be the most comfortable to most officials because it's the same switch as if it were a non-shooting foul.

SWITCHING ON FOULS: TRAIL CALLS WITH FREE THROWS

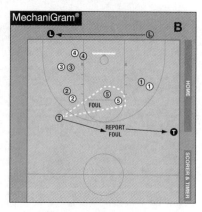

In MechaniGram A, the table-side trail has called a foul that will result in bonus free throws being attempted. The trail will turn to report the foul and then stay in the table-side trail position. The lead will freeze and then proceed to get the players lined up for the ensuing free-throw attempts. Remember to visually confirm the number of attempts and glance at the table for late arriving substitutes before bouncing the ball to the free-throw shooter.

In MechaniGram B, the trail opposite the table has whistled a shooting foul. The trail will move across the court to the reporting area, report the foul and then proceed to the table-side trail position. The lead will move from a table-side position across the line to the lead position opposite the table to administer the free-throw attempts. While the officials will move across the court, they technically will not switch positions.

SWITCHING ON FOULS: NO FREE THROWS

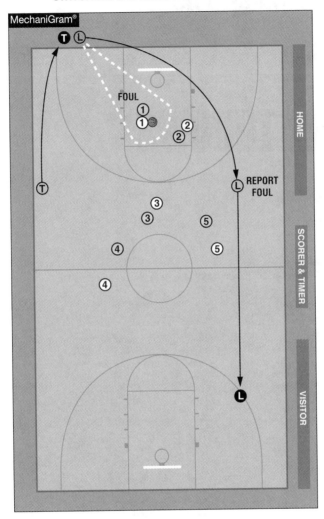

In the MechaniGram, the lead has whistled a rebounding foul in the lane that will not result in free throws. The ball will be inbounded and move down the court. Although it is considered a long-switch situation, the lead and trail will switch positions. The lead will move into the reporting area to report the foul and then proceed downcourt to become the new lead. The trail will move to the new trail position and inbound the ball for the ensuing throw-in.

CREW OF TWO **CHAPTER** 23

FREE THROWS

COVERAGE

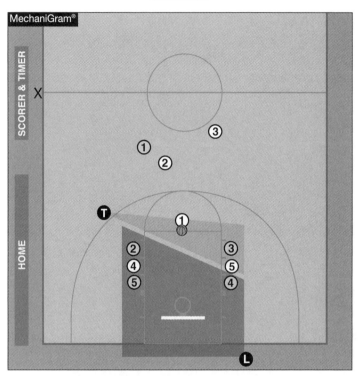

The lead watches players on the opposite lane line (closer to the trail) for potential violations, etc. The lead also watches the lane space nearest the endline on the lane line nearest the lead.

The trail watches players on the opposite lane line (closer to the lead) except the opposite low block area. The trail also watches the free thrower.

The positioning means better coverage of the low-block area opposite the trail.

As shown in the MechaniGram, the trail will have his or her back to the table. The lead should be aware of such and watch for late-breaking substitutions toward the table or timeout requests, prior to administering the free throw.

LEAD MOVEMENT

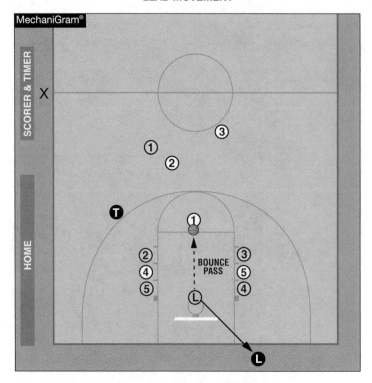

Before administering the free throw, the lead has the ball and is positioned in the lane under the basket. Look for late-arriving substitutes at the scorer's table and beckon them in if appropriate. Signal the number of remaining free throws to the players in the lane and the free thrower. Simultaneously verbalize the number of free throws. Before bouncing the ball to the free thrower, make sure there are no players moving into or leaving lane spaces.

When the free thrower is ready to catch the ball, bounce the ball to the free thrower.

The NFHS manual states that the lead is positioned "approximately four feet from the nearer lane line well off the endline." That position is maintained regardless of the number of free throws. Simply because the players have moved up along the free-throw line does not mean the lead official should now stand in the now vacant bottom space.

After the shot is airborne, adjust your position along the endline a step or two to get a good angle on strong-side rebounding.

TRAIL MOVEMENT

MechaniGram®

SCORER & TIMER

HOME

Do not come into the lane to administer the free throw; the lead administers all free throws.

Pick up the visible 10-second count with the arm farthest from the basket. Using your outside arm ensures the wrist flick doesn't distract the shooter and shows the count clearly to bench personnel, etc. When showing a visible count as a trail during a free-throw attempt, the count should be less demonstrative than your normal visible count so as to not distract the shooter and draw unnecessary attention to the official.

On the last free throw, use the "stop the clock" signal with open hand raised directly above the head immediately after the shooter releases the shot. Use the same arm (furthest from the basket) to ensure the timer clearly sees the signal. During the flight of the try and with your arm still raised, penetrate slightly toward the endline using a two-step crossover move. That movement ensures good angles on rebounding action. If the shot is good, lower your arm. If the shot is no good and the ball is to remain live, use the "start the clock" signal as soon as the ball is touched by or touches a player.

There is no need to signal a made free throw.

TECHNICAL FOUL ADMINISTRATION

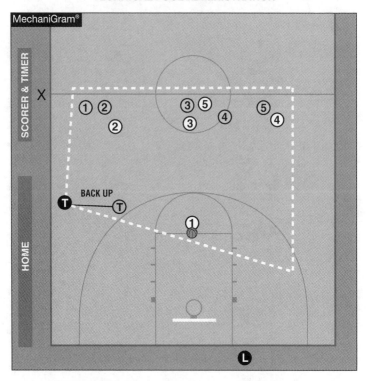

Technical foul administration is one area of coverage where things seem to vary greatly in different state and local associations and different leagues.

In NFHS mechanics, the calling official will assume the trail position near the table. If a confrontational situation is apparent, the calling official may go opposite to assume the lead position and administer the free throws.

Referee recommendation: If the technical foul was called on a player who did something unsportsmanlike toward an opponent and those players remain on the floor during the free throws, let the lead administer the free throws alone while the trail moves toward the division line to watch those players. Having a presence near the division line may be enough to stop the problem.

When the trail remains near the free-throw line, back up farther toward the sideline than you normally would to ensure you see all players near the division line. There's no need to be in tight like during a normal free throw because there are no players along the lane line. The trail's primary responsibility is the remaining nine players and the benches; secondary responsibility is the free thrower. You're simply playing the odds. You're more likely to have problems among the other players or the benches than you are to have a violation on the free thrower.

Discuss the procedures in your pregame with your partner so technical foul free-throw administration runs smoothly.

CREW OF TWO **CHAPTER** 24

SUBSTITUTIONS

- **HANDLING SUBSTITUTIONS: HALFCOURT** P. 206
- **HANDLING SUBSTITUTIONS: TRANSITION** P. 207

HANDLING SUBTITUTIONS: HALFCOURT

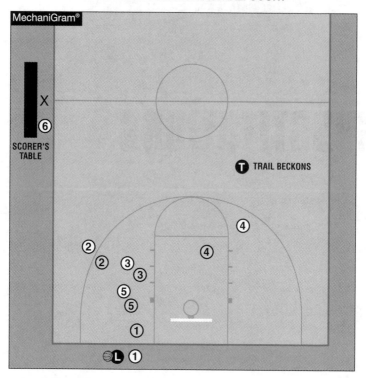

The official near the table, typically the trail, will acknowledge and beckon substitutes onto the court.

Both officials count all players before putting the ball back in play.

On a foul, report the foul before beckoning substitutes. Hold the substitutes at the table until the calling official has completed the reporting procedure. The new nearer official should either beckon the subs or hold them at the table if there will be multiple free throws.

A note on blowing the whistle when beckoning substitutes: Some officials blow the whistle while beckoning on every substitution.

Proponents say the whistle along with the beckoning motion gets the substitute's attention faster, making for a quicker substitution. The whistle along with the stop sign lets your partner know you've got a substitute.

Opponents say the whistle draws unnecessary attention to the official.

Referee recommendation: Blow your whistle. It will alert your partner and save the crew from putting the ball in play before a substitution process has been completed.

HANDLING SUBSTITUTIONS: TRANSITION

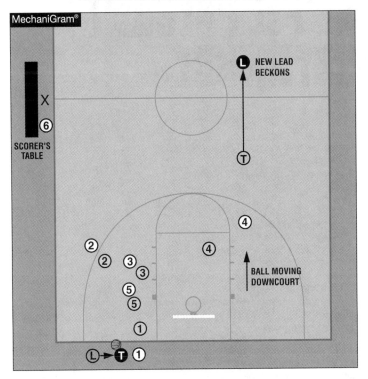

The official near the table should beckon in the substitute. In the MechaniGram, the old trail is moving to the new lead position down the court. While passing the table, the horn sounds and the new lead should stop and beckon in the substitutes. Since the new trail is busy preparing for the ensuing inbound throw-in and on the other side of the court, it makes perfect sense the new lead to handle the substitution process. Even though a horn will sound, blow your whistle so that the new trail is aware that a substitution is still in progress. Keep your hand up and make yourself visible until both teams have the appropriate five players on the court. Then put your hand down and proceed to your new lead position (assuming it is not a press situation).

SAMPLE PREGAME CONFERENCE

A. Pregame floor duties.
 1. Position during warmup.
 2. Count players.
 3. Check equipment, including uniforms.

B. Table duties.
 1. Referee.
  a. Fix table problems early, before 10-minute mark.
  b. Establish rapport with table personnel.
  c. Check scorebook for number of players and duplicate names, numbers.
  d. Check clock/ball.
  e. Check alternating-possession (A/P) arrow.
  f. Ask scorer to help hold substitutes for official's beckon.
  g. Inform table personnel of pertinent rule changes, timing concerns, etc.
 2. Umpire(s)
  a. Watch both teams

C. Captains' and coaches' meeting
 1. Ask players for questions.
 2. All players will exhibit good sportsmanship throughout the contest.
 3. Keep it brief.

D. Return to pregame floor duty position.
 1. Watch players; switch sides.
 2. Relax and begin final mental preparations.

E. Jump ball.
 1. Position, mechanics.
 2. Trail checks the arrow.

F. Court coverage
 1. Lead position.
  a. Concentrate on primary (post play).
  b. Move along endline to create angles (ball side).
  c. Stay with the shooter if in your area.
  d. Rebounding coverage.
 2. Center position. **[THREE-PERSON ONLY]**
  a. Don't become second trail.
  b. Concentrate on primary.
  c. Penetrate toward endline on a try.
  d. Stay with the shooter if in your area.

     e. Goaltending/basket interference responsibilities.
     f. Rebounding coverage
     g. Don't bail out on try.
  3. Trail position.
     a. Concentrate on primary.
     b. Penetrate toward endline on a try.
     c. Stay with the shooter if in your area.
     d. Goaltending/basket interference responsibilities.
     e. Rebounding coverage.
     f. Don't bail out on try.
  4. Adjust to defensive pressure.
     a. Halfcourt pressure.
     b. Fullcourt pressure.

G. Rotating
  1. Lead initiates.
  2. Center initiates.
  3. Coverage areas during rotation.
  4. Rotations started but not completed.

H. Transition.
  1. After turnover.
  2. Center bumped to lead.
  3. Traps in transition.

I. Throw-ins
  1. Coverage areas.
  2. Eye contact.
  3. Trail chops on frontcourt endline throw-ins.
  4. Check for substitutes.
  5. When to use bounce pass.

J. Reporting fouls and and switching
TWO-PERSON
  1. Switch on all fouls not involving free throws.
  2. Calling official table side on foul involving free throws, option to lead if confrontational.
THREE-PERSON
  1. Calling official goes table side, has option of going opposite.
  2. Switch after foul is reported.
  3. No switch on certain backcourt fouls.

K. Free-throw administration.
  1. Two-Person: Lead check table for substitutes.
  2. Three-Person: Trail near 28-foot mark.

L. Timing counts, timeouts
  1. Reporting timeout to table.
  2. Where to stand.

M. Substitutions, disqualifications.
1. Who beckons substitutes.
2. Passing substitutions to partners.
3. Informing coach of disqualification — calling or non-calling official.

N. Rule changes.

O. Rules points of emphasis.

P. Mechanics points of emphasis.

Q. Bench decorum

R. Last-second shot
1. Two-Person: Trail.
2. Three-Person: Official opposite the table.
3. Remind each other of duties oncourt if situation permits.

S. Communication.
1. Shooters.
2. Double whistles.
3. Warnings.
4. Help calls.

HALFTIME

A. Check alternating-possession arrow before leaving floor.

B. Relax.

C. Discuss concerns/problems.

D. Adjustments, if necessary
1. Court coverage.
2. Philosophy: Are the points of emphasis under control?

E. Review overtime procedure.

F. Remind each other of the things done well in first half.

G. Return to floor.
1. Watch players.
2. Just before throw-in, check with table personnel for questions/concerns.

POSTGAME

A. Leave floor together.

B. Relax.

C. Review game.
1. Points of emphasis?
2. Tempo?
3. Bench decorum?
4. Strange plays, rulings?

D. Solicit constructive criticism — "What could I have done better?"

E. Leave facility together — there's safety in numbers.

F. Reports.

WOA Officials Receive a 7-1/2% Discount Year Round

Gerry Davis Sports is proud to provide WOA basketball officials with all their officiating apparel, equipment and supplies such as:

Davis Basketball Pants

Adjusting Track

Waistband Clip

List Price = $49.90   WOA Price = $46.16

Ultra-Mesh Basketball Shirts

**List Price = $29.90
WOA Price = $27.66**

Reebok Zig Energy Shoes

Patent Leather or Matte Finish

**List Price = $99.90
WOA Price = $92.41**

Gerry Davis Sports

2420 W. Nordale Drive, Appleton, WI 54914
Order Phone: 800-916-9088 • Business Phone: 920-830-3140
Web Site: www.gerrydavis.com • Email: safe@gerrydavis.com

Hours of operation: Monday through Friday – 7:30 AM to 5:00 PM CST
24-Hour ordering is available through our web page: www.gerrydavis.com

Great Products + Great Prices + Great Service = A Great Call!

Aflac is an extra measure of financial protection.

When you're sick or hurt, Aflac pays cash benefits directly to you, unless otherwise assigned, to help you and your family with unexpected expenses.

For more information about policy benefits, limitations, and exclusions, please call your Aflac insurance agent:

Steve Pohlman
2073 211th Ave NE
Sammamish, WA 98074
206.310.9981
steven_pohlman@us.aflac.com

We've got you under our wing.®